THE GRAB BAG BOOK

THE GRAB BAG BOOK

Your Ultimate Guide to Liferaft Survival

Frances & Michael Howorth

PARADISE CAY PUBLICATIONS

Published in the United States by
Paradise Cay Publications
PO Box 29, Arcata, California 95518-0029
www.paracay.com
707-822-9063 PH
707-822-9163 FX

ISBN 0939837-53-6

A CIP catalogue record for this book is available from the British Library.

Note: While all reasonable care has been taken in the publication of this book,
the publishers take no responsibility for the use of the methods or products
described in the book.

A & C Black uses paper produced with elemental chlorine-free pulp,
harvested from managed sustainable forests.

Typeset in Stone Sans 9/11 pt
Printed and bound in Great Britain by Cromwell Press, Trowbridge, Wiltshire

CONTENTS

4 ABANDONING SHIP

5 INITIAL AND SUBSEQUENT ACTIONS IN THE LIFERAFT

6 LONG-TERM SURVIVAL IN A LIFERAFT

7 INITIAL FIRST AID AND EMERGENCY TREATMENT

8 AILMENTS

9 RESCUE

APPENDIX

AUTHORS' NOTE

Throughout this book the word 'skipper' is used to describe the person in charge of the boat. The skipper is not necessarily the owner of the vessel, though he may be.

The use of the masculine and feminine pronoun is arbitrary. It does not indicate that one gender or another is preferred or desired for any particular job or function.

This book is written especially for those who sail aboard pleasure vessels of any size, whether sail, motor or both. A pleasure vessel of 13.7 m (45 ft) or more in length is classified as a Class XII vessel in the UK. Yachts that cease to be 'pleasure vessels' and/or Class XII vessels are subject to different legal requirements and codes of practice. Those regulations are not taken into account in this book and must be reviewed before any safety equipment is purchased.

This book complies with the International Maritime Organisation (IMO) resolution A.657(16).

Our thanks to:

Steven Huxley, MRCC Falmouth
Brian Mulland, Inmarsat
Charlie Mill, Ocean Safety
Anselm Fabiq, Navtec
Dennis London, ACR
MCA Information Centre, Southampton
Malcolm Dunning, lecturer in Marine Law, Warsash
Commander Dee Norton, Chief of SAR Policy, USCG
Fl Lt John Williamson, Manager, RAF Kinloss
Sgt Robson on ASRA equipment
Sgt G P Quilliam on Nimrod SAR operations
Surgeon Commander Geraldine Salmon, P & O Princess Cruises
McMurdo Ltd.

1

BEING PREPARED

Common yachting folklore warns us all against thinking about a disaster at sea on the basis that if you do, it is sure to happen. But as the skipper of a yacht you must be prepared for every eventuality and it is your duty to make sure all your crew are too.

This book is all about:
- Surviving the disaster of abandoning ship.
- Being mentally and physically prepared for the sailor's ultimate nightmare.
- Why you need to supplement the equipment found inside your liferaft.
- Selecting equipment for your grab bag.

It is **NOT** about:
- The particular brand of liferaft or EPIRB you should buy.
- Dealing with the accident or emergency that caused the disaster.

It is written for:
- Skipper and crew aboard any private vessel.
- Any size or type of boat.
- Any voyage from across the bay to around the world.

PROPER PREPARATION AND TRAINING

As a responsible skipper, part of the planning for a passage includes ensuring the correct safety equipment is carried aboard your yacht. It is not easy to part with hard earned money for an item of equipment that you doubt will be used, and may even be thrown away after a few years still unopened. It *is* easy to cut corners at the purchasing stage and buy only the barest minimum. Sadly, when the

1

unimaginable catastrophe happens it will probably be too late to go back and purchase that safety item you previously rejected as an unnecessary expense.

The danger is greater the further you go offshore, because of the higher risk of being at sea in rough weather, but at least you cannot run aground in the middle of an ocean. A shipwreck, however, can happen anywhere, at any time, through no one's fault. If you do have to take to your liferaft, what can you do to improve your chances of being rescued, without injury or loss of life? Read this book at your passage-planning stage to decide what to select for your emergency bag – and store this book in your grab bag so you will have it with you in the liferaft.

The importance of training cannot be emphasised enough. This book should be read by every crewmember, re-read regularly, and used for training exercises. Research has shown that at the moment when disaster strikes 75 per cent of people will be stunned and bewildered. Those who have been trained to expect and to cope with such situations will fall back on well-learned patterns of behaviour. A trained crew will work together to leave the yacht safely, carrying with them the maximum equipment to aid their survival.

It is vital that the skipper demonstrates strong leadership and appropriate action both before and after abandonment. It would be nice to think that once you are safely aboard your liferaft, your worst troubles are over and you will be rescued almost immediately. With modern communications, help may be on its way, but you still have to survive until it arrives. What is already packed inside your liferaft and what you additionally take with you are your keys to survival.

Remember: *no one is a survivor until they have been rescued or have reached safety by their own efforts.*

LIFERAFT EMERGENCY PACKS

Horror stories about the survival gear found in liferafts abound. It's not just a question of the lack of equipment or the missing items, but also the quality of the supplies. Even in the best of liferafts the supplies included are limited. It all comes down to money and weight: the more supplies that are packed with a liferaft, the heavier it is, the larger the outer container needed and the more expensive it becomes. Most rafts for the leisure market are sold with a choice of packs, with the most basic and cheapest being a selection of simple items to maintain the raft – and not necessarily of high quality. Pray you never have to survive for long with just a basic pack.

WHY YOU NEED A GRAB BAG

Even in the best situation for abandoning ship, when you have a little time, these precious minutes are far more likely to be spent trying to save your yacht rather than choosing what to take with you.

You are unlikely to be in the best frame of mind to make sensible decisions, nor will you necessarily have the equipment that will aid you best in a liferaft, unless you have thought about it while alongside and were able to go shopping.

Your grab bag should contain everything essential to your survival in a liferaft. If you do not have a liferaft and propose to use your dinghy in an emergency, it is even more important to have some form of abandon ship bag, as your dinghy is unlikely to have even the most basic of emergency supplies.

YOUR YACHT AND ITS EQUIPMENT

No two situations are ever the same, but if a yacht is sinking there is one overriding priority: the saving of life. It is too late at this point to discover that the liferaft is out of date for a service, the EPIRB is registered in the name of another yacht and the spare flares were landed last weekend.

Good seamanship, knowledge and common sense will help ensure safety at sea. With planning and forethought many a disaster can be prevented, but sadly not all. The training needed by you and your crew, together with the equipment you choose for your yacht depends, to a large extent, on the areas in which you sail or plan to sail, the weather conditions you are likely to encounter and, to a much lesser extent, upon the size of your yacht. A large yacht may need more of, or a larger size of, some equipment than her smaller sister, but most of the items will be identical if they are sailing in the same areas.

When replacing VHF radios, ensure that they are GMDSS compliant.

RADIO AND AN OVERVIEW OF GMDSS

Since 1999, when GMDSS (Global Maritime Distress and Safety System) became worldwide, going to sea has been much safer. It is now much more likely that a yacht in distress will receive assistance and that time spent by crew in a liferaft will be much shorter. You are much more likely to be hours, rather than days, awaiting rescue. No longer does a lack of VHF contact before abandoning ship mean your chance of rescue in a remote area is minimal.

GMDSS is primarily a vessel-to-shore signalling system, where a vessel in distress can alert a land-based Rescue Co-ordination Centre (RCC), which then co-ordinates the rescue. It is an international system using terrestrial and satellite technology together with shipboard radio systems, ensuring that vessels can communicate wherever they are in the world with shore stations and other ships. The equipment does not require specialist radio operators, and an important part of the system is the automatic way in which it transmits and receives distress alerts, either using conventional radio or the Inmarsat satellite system. GMDSS is not just for emergency and distress messages; it is also used for Urgency broadcasts and routine ship-to-ship and ship-to-shore communications.

GMDSS is not simply a more expensive radio that calls and listens on designated frequencies and saves the authorities from listening out on special distress frequencies: it is a complete system with several elements, including satellite communication, weather and navigation information, and VHF, MF and HF radiotelephony. It also embraces secondary distress signalling devices, which include Search And Rescue Transponders (SARTs) and Emergency Position Indicating Radio Beacons (EPIRBs).

At present, it is not compulsory for a small private yacht to carry GMDSS equipment, but all boats should include some if not all of the elements of the system. The decision about which of the elements to fit will depend upon the nature of that yacht's voyaging.

EMERGENCY POSITION INDICATING RADIO BEACON (EPIRB)

An EPIRB is a radio distress signalling device designed to automatically provide a distress message and locating signal. They have been in use since the 1980s and all vessels required to carry GMDSS, regardless of the sea area they sail in, must carry EPIRBs. It is probably the most important piece of equipment to pack in your grab bag.

Since EPIRBs were first introduced (up to 31 December 2001) 12,871 people had been rescued following an EPIRB alert.

One sailor who owes his life to an EPIRB is Pablo Pirenack. He left the USA to fulfil a lifelong ambition to sail a small yacht singlehanded across the Atlantic. He got more than he bargained for when Hurricane Alberto battered his 8-metre yacht to bits in August 2000 and he took to his liferaft. It was his EPIRB that saved him, by enabling a gas tanker to come to his rescue just 26 hours after he first hit the transmit button. His story, published in the yachting press, is a salutary lesson to one and all who cross the seas in small craft. It is the same lesson taught by Lord Baden-Powell when he set up the Scout movement with the motto 'Be Prepared'. Now the yachtsman's motto should be: *Be Prepared – Be EPIRBed.*

LESSONS LEARNED FROM DISASTERS

Two yacht races have had a major impact on safety: the 1979 Fastnet Race and the 1998 Sydney–Hobart Yacht Race. The Fastnet disaster, which cost the lives of 15 sailors, caused a major upheaval in yacht design in the 1980s. The Sydney–Hobart tragedy cost six lives, and the findings of John Abernethy, the Australian Coroner, are still having repercussions. The recommendations of that coroner, though intended for racing boats, should be considered by any cruising yacht when selecting safety equipment. They included the requirement that all:

- Crew wear a personal EPIRB when on deck in all weather conditions.
- Crew are trained in the use of personal EPIRBs.
- Yachts carry on board a 406 MHz EPIRB and not a 121.5 MHz EPIRB.
- Yachts' batteries be of the closed or gel cell type.
- Crew who are on deck during rough weather should wear clothing that will protect them from hypothermia.
- Crew use personal flotation devices (PFDs) other than the 'Mae West' type lifejackets.
- Crew have with them a personal strobe light when on deck in all weather conditions.

The Coroner gave further recommendations concerning liferafts and training, which are included in the next chapter.

SHORESIDE PREPARATION

Even with the most comprehensive communications equipment, a distress call may be unsuccessful in attracting attention or providing enough information for the rescue services. It is vital that someone ashore knows where you are sailing and what survival equipment you carry. If you are sailing in British waters, fill in The Voluntary Safety Identification Scheme Form (CG66) available from the MCA (Maritime and Coastguard Agency) website and keep a copy for your records. It will provide HM Coastguard with details of your boat in a Search and Rescue situation. Ensure the form is updated should any details change and that your shoreside contact is likely to be available and is able to play his part whilst you are sailing. Before any passage fill in a Voyage Details Plan (see Appendix 1) and give it to your nominated shoreside contact. It will contain all the details they need to help set in motion a Search and Rescue, in the event of your yacht failing to arrive at her destination at the expected time.

2

YOUR LIFERAFT AND IT'S CONTENTS

A liferaft is designed as a last resort, to keep the crew of a boat alive after their vessel has sunk, until help arrives. It should provide environmental protection even in rough seas, and aid location by creating a larger target for the rescuers to find. It can never be as comfortable as your yacht, but it should be a lot better than floating in the water supported by a lifejacket. A liferaft should never be used unless it is certain that the boat herself cannot be saved. It is not a better refuge than a boat, nor can it be considered safer in rough seas than the much larger parent vessel. Remember the old adage: *Never step down into a liferaft.*

CHOOSING A LIFERAFT

Liferaft manufacturers do not make things easy. There is no standard for classification of liferafts for non-commercial craft, and it is extremely hard to make a like-for-like comparison. While one liferaft may be more expensive than another, this may be due to the survival pack contents rather than the construction of the raft. It is extremely unlikely that you will get the chance to test a range of liferafts, and unless you go to a boat show you will probably be buying blind, trusting to a salesman or the manufacturer's reputation. Worst of all you will, in all likelihood, be parting with your money to buy something you will never see open until the first service.

A liferaft can be priceless or useless, depending on the circumstances.

Various organisations have laid down standards of manufacture, design and equipment to be carried in liferafts.

The International Maritime Organisation (IMO) have, in their Safety Of Life At Sea convention, known as SOLAS, created the highest. The Royal Ocean Racing Club (RORC), together with the Offshore Racing Council (ORC), have produced the next highest standard required by pleasure craft engaged in racing. For American boaters the officiating body is the United States Coast Guard (USCG).

Buying any liferaft is all about choices. Sea conditions can be as rough close to shore as in the middle of the ocean. The main difference when going further afield is not the quality or style of your liferaft but the need to carry more survival gear.

- Should you choose a SOLAS, RORC/ORC or USCG specified model?
- Would the cheapest model be sufficient?
- What size do you select?
- Should it be stored in a container or a valise?
- Which survival pack do you buy?
- What about renting instead of buying?

LIFERAFT TYPES

There are five main types of survival craft used aboard private vessels:

Inflatable dinghy

- Can be pressed into service in an emergency.
- Only of use if stored inflated on deck.
- Always second best.
- Only really useful in very calm conditions.
- Frequently capsizes and floats inverted in heavy seas.

Dual-purpose tender/liferaft

- Special tender manufactured to convert to liferaft use.
- A survival pack adds a canopy and automatic inflation.
- As expensive as some stand-alone liferafts.
- To change from one function to another is time consuming.

Inshore liferaft

- Not a real liferaft.
- Either a simple rescue platform: a flat, unballasted disk that can hold crew out of the water, drier than treading water.
- Or a more protective rescue pod: more like a liferaft, minimal equipment, ballast and space.
- Suitable only for use on inland waters or within very protected bays.

Coastal liferaft

- Cheaper and lighter than most offshore rafts.
- Not made to ORC (Ocean Racing Council) standards.
- Often consists of only one tube with much reduced ballast.
- May have an upgradeable emergency pack for longer passages.
- Manufactured on sometimes false assumption that, close to shore, help will come quickly.
- Does not meet the more rigorous requirements of an offshore model.

Offshore liferaft

- Offers the highest specifications.
- Includes two independent stacked flotation chambers for redundancy, greater freeboard and comfort of the occupants.
- Self-erecting canopy for protection.
- Plenty of ballast to keep it upright.
- RORC/ORC liferafts are all offshore models.
- An offshore liferaft that meets ORC specifications is suitable for all areas of use.

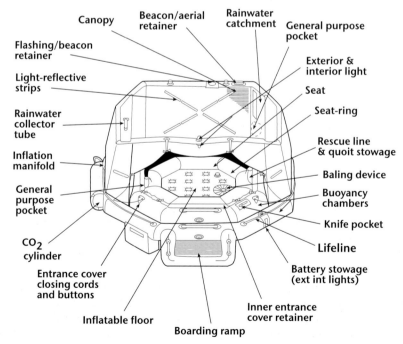

SOLAS rafts have the highest specification of all.

SOLAS LIFERAFT

Leaving aside money and weight, the best liferaft will always be a SOLAS-compliant model. A statement made by the Coroner following the disastrous 1998 Sydney–Hobart Race should be considered when choosing a raft:

'The recommendation of a liferaft complying with the SOLAS requirements is not, as one submission states, for "A possible slight gain in people comfort in the unusual circumstance of a crew having to take to the raft". It is so that if the unusual circumstance does arise, the crew will have the best opportunity of survival and they are entitled to that.'

SIZE AND POSITION

The size of your liferaft should be based on the maximum number of crew who sail aboard your yacht. Yacht liferafts are supplied in four, six, eight and ten-man sizes. There is a good case for buying a raft that is intended for two persons more than your expected crew, to give more room, as long as the raft is well ballasted.

Unfortunately a half-empty raft is more likely to capsize because part of the ballast comes from the weight of the crew. If your boat sleeps 8 but you never sail with more than 4 people aboard, then a 6-person liferaft is probably the largest you should buy.

If a liferaft is to be of use in an emergency it must be immediately available, ideally stowed on deck or in a locker that opens from the deck. Linked to the decision on where to locate the raft is choice of container:

A rigid plastic container
- For any liferaft kept on deck, to protect it from weather and knocks.
- Can be too heavy for a small person to move.

A fabric valise
- Lighter, less bulky and slightly cheaper.
- Only if protected from the elements in a deck locker or down below.

If your liferaft is to be fixed vertically, eg to the pushpit or route, you should advise the supplier/service agent as the contents may have to be packed differently.

Many manufacturers now vacuum-bag their liferafts. This protects the raft from water ingress, reduces the size and lengthens the time before the first service is required.

Wherever you eventually choose to stow the liferaft make sure it has inflation instructions clearly written on it, or on an attached waterproof sticker, with the print large enough to be read without glasses. Check that these instructions are clear enough so that even a complete novice can understand them and be able to launch the liferaft correctly.

LIFERAFT EMERGENCY PACKS

In general the cheaper the liferaft the less equipment is included. Fig 1 lists the contents of four standardised emergency packs available for liferafts, together with a list recommended by the Coroner after the Sydney-Hobart Race tragedy in 1998. Manufacturers generally offer a choice of packs and will include virtually anything else you want, for a price of course. Unfortunately, the more you include inside the liferaft the bigger and heavier the container or valise must be and the more expensive it becomes. The most basic emergency equipment includes only items to repair the raft, but even the most comprehensive SOLAS 'A' pack will need to be augmented with a grab bag.

Liferaft packs are generally stored inside a waterproof bag attached within the raft to prevent everything coming loose upon launching and inflation. The knife for cutting the painter is stowed separately as are such items as a drogue and a rescue quoit.

ADDITIONS TO YOUR LIFERAFT

It is worth considering storing some of your extra items inside the liferaft, especially if the supplied emergency pack included is very sparse. This decision is best made when you purchase a new raft, as it may require a larger container to hold everything, but it can also be done at service time. The advantage is obviously that you know the gear will be with your liferaft. The downside is that it will make the raft heavier and you need to be sure that the lightest and weakest crewmember will still be able to launch the raft.

Do not pack your primary EPIRB inside the liferaft. Abandoning ship is not the only time you or your crew may need to set off the EPIRB and it would be extremely awkward to have to inflate your liferaft to operate the beacon. But a second EPIRB packed inside the liferaft is an excellent idea. An EPIRB is the single most important item of survival equipment that you can have in your liferaft to communicate with the world. Survival is necessary but the ultimate aim is to be rescued quickly.

SERVICING YOUR LIFERAFT

Servicing is expensive but necessary, and extending the period between services only makes it more likely that the raft will require more expensive repairs later or even be condemned early. Servicing should be undertaken for three reasons:
- To replace dated items like flares, batteries and water.
- To inspect for water damage and make sure the inflation cylinder is full.
- To check the raft for wear, particularly at the folds.

Standard Liferaft Emergency Packs

RORC/ORC PACK	Sydney–Hobart 1998 recommendations	OffShore Pack – Type E	SOLAS B PACK (up to 12 person size)	SOLAS A PACK (up to 12 person size)
Leisure/Racing Yachtsmen	*Offshore Racing*	*Leisure/Cruising Yachtsmen*	*Leisure/Commercial Coastal*	*Leisure/Commercial Offshore*
Bailer	Bailer	Bailer	Bailer	Bailer
Hand flare x 3	Hand flare x 4	Hand flare x 3	Hand flare x 3	Hand flare x 6
Paddle x 2	Paddle x 2	Paddle x 2	Paddle x 2	Paddle x 2
Pump	Pump	Pump	Pump	Pump
Repair kit	Repair kit	Repair kit	Repair kit	Repair kit
Rescue line and quoit	Rescue line and quoit	Rescue line and quoit	Rescue line and quoit	Rescue line and quoit
Safety knife	Safety knife	Safety knife	Safety knife	Safety knife
Sea anchor	Sea anchor	Sea anchor	Sea anchor x 2	Sea anchor x 2
Signal card (SOLAS 2)	Signal card (SOLAS 2)	Signal card (SOLAS 2)	Signal card (SOLAS 2)	Signal card (SOLAS 2)
Sponge x 2	Sponge (1pp)	Sponge x 2	Sponge x 2	Sponge x 2
Survival instructions	Survival instructions	Survival instructions	Survival instructions	Survival instructions
Flashlight (waterproof)	Flashlight (waterproof)	Flashlight (waterproof)	Flashlight (waterproof)	Flashlight (waterproof)
+ spare batteries and bulb	+ spare batteries and bulb	+ spare batteries and bulb	+ spare batteries and bulb	+ spare batteries and bulb
Whistle	Whistle	Whistle	Whistle	Whistle
Anti-seasickness tablets (6pp)	Anti-seasickness tablets (6pp)	Anti-seasickness tablets (6pp)	Anti-seasickness tablets (6pp)	Anti-seasickness tablets (6pp)
Plus	*Plus*	*Plus*	*Plus*	*Plus*
Parachute flare x 2	Parachute flare x 2	Parachute flare x 2	Parachute flare x 2	Parachute flare x 4
First aid kit	First aid kit	First aid kit	First aid kit	First aid kit
Signalling mirror	Signalling mirror	Signalling mirror	Signalling mirror	Signalling mirror
	Fishing kit	Graduated drinking cup		Graduated drinking cup
	Buoyant smoke signal x 2	Fishing kit	Buoyant smoke signal x 1	Fishing kit
		Radar reflector or SART	Radar reflector or SART	Buoyant smoke signal x 2
			Seasick bags (1pp)	
			Thermal protective aids x 2	Seasick bags (1pp)
	Drinking water (0.5 l per person)	Drinking water (0.5 l per person)		Thermal protective aids x 2
	Food ration			Can opener x 3
				Scissors
	Sunburn cream x 2			Drinking water 1.5 l per person)
	Plastic bags (5pp)			Food ration
	Buoyancy tube leak plug x 6			(10,000 kJ per person)

Always choose a service centre that will allow you and your crew to be present, so you can watch as your raft is opened. This may be the only chance you ever get to see your raft and personally check its equipment before you need to use it.

RENTING A RAFT

If you normally sail or race in confined waters, buying a liferaft may seem an unnecessary expense for your annual holiday trip further afield or for an offshore race. Renting a liferaft can be a good option and it is possible to rent for as short a time as a weekend or for as long as a year or more. The same care must be taken with choosing a rented liferaft as with a purchased model. Ensure you know exactly what the emergency pack contains, so you know how much you need to pack in your grab bag to supplement it. Always check that the rental raft was serviced immediately prior to your hiring, so you know it is in good condition and contains everything listed.

TRAINING

Again and again, following maritime disasters, the benefits of training and attending courses in sea survival are cited. It has been proven that if a response has been well learned, the human brain no longer requires deliberation at time of crisis. Instead, it has only to select between a set of pre-learned responses. One of the formal recommendations made by the Coroner after the 1998 Sydney–Hobart Race was that at least 50 per cent of the crew of every competing yacht should have completed a yacht safety and survival course every three years. This is good advice for the crew of any yacht.

3

YOUR GRAB BAG AND ITS CONTENTS

To decide what to pack in your grab bag you must first answer the following questions:

- What is contained in my liferaft?
- What is the quality of the equipment?
- Where will the boat be sailing?
- What is the maximum crew number aboard?

Perhaps a grab bag is best viewed as life insurance, with you and your crew as the immediate beneficiaries. It's just a matter of deciding on the premium you are willing to pay for the lives of yourself and your crew. Sadly, assembling a comprehensive grab bag will not be cheap. Some items will last almost forever and others will need to be replaced at regular intervals.

CHOOSING A CONTAINER

Choosing the right container for your grab bag is somewhat of a chicken and egg situation. Do you decide what you want when you abandon ship and choose a bag to fit it all? Or do you select the bag to fit the stowage position you have in mind and see how much you can fit in? A soft dry bag is easier to handle and live with in a liferaft, but a rigid waterproof box can be towed to provide more space.

There are certain common properties that every grab bag should have regardless of how large or small:

Every grab bag should be:
- Brightly coloured ideally, waterproof and able to float.
- Clearly marked with the name of your yacht and the words 'GRAB BAG'.
- Fitted with a lanyard to attach it to the liferaft.
- Duplicated to match the number of liferafts carried.

Inside the bag:

- Shape a domestic polyethylene cutting board to fit the base to reinforce the bottom of a soft bag and prevent sagging. This will be useful for cutting things whilst in the raft.
- Use closed-cell foam for cushioning and extra flotation.
- Seal individual items in waterproof plastic bags.
- Use a vacuum-bagging machine to seal and reduce size to a minimum.
- Store small items in plastic boxes or jars with secure lids.
- List the contents of all sealed items on the outside with waterproof ink.
- Include any equipment instructions on waterproof paper.
- Attach a lanyard to everything to prevent loss, especially in rough weather.
- Cover anything with a sharp point that could puncture your raft, eg tip of gaff.

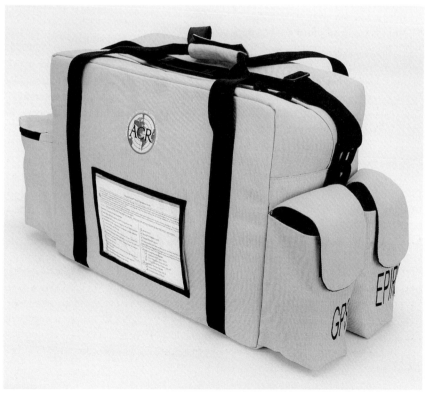

Purpose-made grab bags like this one are widely available.

Once the bag is chosen and filled check it will still float. Stow the bag on deck or close by, ideally in the cockpit on a sailboat or the wheelhouse on a motorboat.

Every crewmember must know exactly where the grab bag lives and what it contains. They should also be able to handle the fully laden bag (if necessary consider splitting the load into two smaller bags).

Whatever you decide it will probably be a compromise – the bag from the movie *Mary Poppins* would be perfect as it was much bigger inside than out. Try to pack the bag so that items likely to be needed first, like the maintenance and protection equipment, are at the top. If you have decided to split the load into two bags and cannot stow them both in an ideal spot, you will have to prioritize or split items. An empty spare bag, kept handy, is a good idea to use for stowing some of your Last Minute Grabs.

WHAT TO PACK IN YOUR GRAB BAG

The rest of this chapter details suggested items to pack in your grab bag. These have been divided into a series of categories:
• Search and Rescue
• Maintenance and Protection
• Medical
• Food and Drink
• Survival and Morale
• Personal
• Miscellaneous
• Last Minute Grabs

Except for Last Minute Grabs, the categories are in order of priority but the items listed within are purely in alphabetical order. *Items marked with an asterisk* are those you would find in most comprehensive standard emergency liferaft packs, such as SOLAS 'A'.*

SEARCH AND RESCUE EQUIPMENT

This category almost ties for first place with Maintenance and Protection, but because achieving rescue is what you want more than anything else, it wins by a short head. A liferaft is extremely difficult to spot especially in rough seas. The more you can do in your liferaft to attract attention and the more methods of signalling you have available, the more likely it is that someone will come to your aid. The more items you have in this category, the less you should need of other categories.

EPIRB

An EPIRB is a small, portable, battery-powered transmitter that sends out an emergency signal to rescue services. This device is probably **the most important piece of equipment that you can take in a liferaft.** Even though you may already have made contact by radio, your EPIRB will help the Search and Rescue authorities (SAR) home in on your position. Carrying an EPIRB will make up for a great many other deficiencies your grab bag might suffer from, and it will almost certainly ensure you spend only hours in a liferaft rather than weeks. The only thing better than an EPIRB when you need it is a second EPIRB as a back up!

There are, at present, three main types of EPIRB, each using differing technologies and different radio frequencies: 121.5 MHz, 406 MHz and Inmarsat E. All EPIRBs transmit on internationally recognised distress frequencies that can be monitored by SAR aircraft and vessels, land stations and selected satellites, though not all units have the same capabilities or utilise the same systems.

121.5 MHz EPIRB

These beacons are the least expensive EPIRBs, but they utilise the oldest technology. These have a number of major problems, including lack of global coverage, and from 1 February 2009 satellites will cease to monitor them. They are ideal as a personal man overboard alert but are of limited use to the offshore, safety-conscious sailor as a primary EPIRB and cannot be registered.

The 121.5 MHz frequency is, however, still important as a homing signal. It is fitted as an auxiliary, low-powered transmitter into many 406 MHz and Inmarsat E EPIRBs to enable SAR vessels and any aircraft to home in on the signal. All civil aircraft, especially those on oceanic routes, are required to monitor the 121.5 MHz frequency and much useful corroborative information is reported by over-flying aircraft.

406 MHz EPIRB

These beacons were introduced to take full advantage of the existing communications satellites and give complete global coverage. The newest units include a GPS, enabling accurate information about the location of the beacon to be transmitted and allowing the SAR forces to be mobilised immediately.

Inmarsat E EPIRB

The most recent type of EPIRB, available since 1997 and utilising the latest technology, is the Inmarsat E or L-Band satellite EPIRB using the Inmarsat communications satellites to give global coverage, except in the extreme polar regions. At the time of writing, these units are more expensive than a 406 MHz EPIRB in the UK and are not available in the USA.

Choosing an EPIRB

The table on page 19 offers a guide to some of the advantages and disadvantages of each type. The final decision as to which EPIRB you choose will be a very personal one, but bear in mind the following:

- For busy coastal waters one EPIRB is probably sufficient, especially if you carry a portable VHF and a mobile phone.
- If you are sailing offshore a 121.5 MHz EPIRB is unsuitable because, among other reasons, it cannot be registered so, if activated, will not provide the authorities with your details.
- If you plan to sail far north or south choose a 406 MHz EPIRB.
- If you can afford it buy a GPS 406 MHz and an Inmarsat E, for the speediest rescue in all circumstances and in case of a problem with one system or manufacturer.

Once the assessment has been made and the EPIRB type selected, with or without GPS, there is still a further choice to make:

The EPIRB is the most important piece of equipment that you can take in your liferaft.

Category/Class I – automatic deployment and activation if the EPIRB sinks below 1 to 3 m (3 to 10 ft). Required aboard GMDSS compliant vessels.

Category/Class II – manual operation only.

PLB – Personal Locator Beacon – a smaller unit but with reduced battery life.

For non-GMDSS compliant boats, choosing between the categories is difficult, even without adding a financial factor. At first glance an automatic Category I EPIRB looks best, but:
- It is more expensive.
- It must be mounted on deck and clear of obstacles, so it can float free.
- It must not be underwater whilst sailing, as this could cause activation.
- Sinking involving a dismasting could obscure the unit and prevent it ever floating free.

With these thoughts in mind, and especially if you only purchase one unit, a good choice might be:
- Category II EPIRB in the top of your grab bag on a sailing yacht.
- Category I EPIRB aboard a motor yacht.
- But best of all on any yacht, mount a Category I EPIRB on deck and pack a Category II or PLB in your grab bag.

Whichever choice you make, ensure the unit is handy and that all crewmembers know where it is and how it works. Make sure it is marked with your vessel's name, like all major safety items, in case it becomes separated from your vessel or liferaft. Marked items can give rescuers valuable information about drift rates and the vessel's identity.

Registration
It cannot be emphasised too strongly how important it is to **register every 406 MHz EPIRB**. Fill in and send off the registration card that comes with the beacon. If you have lost the card, details of where to register are in Sources of Supplies and Information in the Appendix.

When an EPIRB is activated these details enable the Coastguard authorities to telephone your listed emergency contact. Your shoreside contact can:
- Provide valuable help to confirm your possible position.
- Rule out the possibility of a false alarm, which sadly still accounts for eight out of nine transmissions.
- Give important extra information from your Voyage Details Plan (see Appendix).

Flashlight/torch*

A waterproof model to be used for signalling is included in all standard liferaft emergency packs, with a spare bulb and batteries.

Even a very small flashlight is extremely effective at night for signalling. Some liferafts have no internal light, so pack a flashlight near the top of your grab bag in case you have to abandon ship at night.

Comparison of Emergency Position Indicating Radio Beacons (EPIRBs)

	121.5 MHz Class A or B 406 MHz	406 MHz Category/Class I or II 406 MHz	406 MHz PLB	Immarsat E
Other additional names	Emergency Locator Beacon/Personal Locator Beacon/Mini B	Emergency Locator Beacon	Personal EPIRB	L-Band EPIRB
Strobe light fitted	no	yes	no	yes
Actual distress frequencies	121.5 MHz + sometimes 243 MHz	406.025 MHz and 406.028 MHz	406.025 MHz and 406.028 MHz	667 channels (300 Hz spacing) at 1645 GHz
Possible or optional additional homing	121.5 MHz	121.5 MHz	121.5 MHz	121.5 MHz or SART
Integral or external GPS option	no	possible	possible	yes
Signal received by satellite	Only until 1 February 2009	yes	yes	yes
Homing by any vessel with radar	no	no	no	yes if SART fitted
Time to receipt of distress at MRCC	Minimum of 6 hours	Average 1 to 2 hours (5 minutes with GPS)	Average 1 to 2 hours (5 minutes with GPS)	2 to 5 minutes
Coverage	30% earth surface, near coast	100% earth surface	100% earth surface	97% earth surface (up to 76N and 76S)
Location accuracy	12.4 miles/20km	3.1 miles/5km (100m with GPS)	3.1 miles/5km (100m with GPS)	100m
Operational battery life at -20°C	24 to 48 hours	48 hours for GMDSS approved units	24 hours	48 hours
Transmission of nature of distress	no	possible	no	possible
Transmission of vessel identification	no	yes, after programming	yes, after programming	yes
GMDSS compliant	no	Cat I yes, Cat II no	no	yes with automatic activation

Class A – float free and automatic turn on
Class B – manual deploy and turn on

Category I – float free and automatic turn on
Category II – manual deploy and turn on

Diving lights are a good choice as they must be waterproof, a floating model is a bonus; make sure you can fit a lanyard. An additional hands-free waterproof light is a plus.

Ensure, if possible, that all flashlights use the same size batteries and pack plenty of spares. Stock rotate all batteries with the yacht's regular supply and include the grab bag flashlights on the list of items to check before a passage.

Kite

A highly visible kite attracts attention and helps rescuers pinpoint your location, plus it's fun to fly! One manufacturer makes a parafoil kite in bright orange with the international distress signal of a black ball and square printed on it. It will fly in winds from 5–25 knots and can even lift a strobe light or radar reflector.

Pyrotechnics/flares

Flares, also called pyrotechnics, are recognised distress signals designed to alert people that you are in trouble and provide a location signal for would-be rescuers to home in on. Ensure that the flares you choose meet SOLAS recommendations. There are other flares on the market that do not meet that standard of burn time or brightness but, if you are in distress, you will want all the signalling power you can get.

An in-date flare kit, stored in a waterproof container where it can be quickly located in an emergency, should be part of every yacht's equipment no matter where you sail. This flare container should be included on your Last Minute Grab list and spare out-of-date flares can be included in your grab bag. Add extra flares to your grab bag if your liferaft emergency pack is deficient or, better still, have them packed inside the liferaft.

A red parachute rocket flare can reach 300 metres and burn brightly for 40 seconds. Ensure that all the crew know how to use flares.

Flares – orange smoke*

SOLAS specification buoyant smoke signals burn for not less than three minutes and will not ignite oil or fuel. They should be carried for all offshore passages. If you never intend to sail far from shore, handheld orange flares, which burn for about one minute, may be sufficient.

Flares – red handheld*

SOLAS specification red handheld flares have a minimum burning period of one minute and a luminous intensity of 15,000 candela; nothing less should be carried. A minimum of three should be carried aboard all yachts and three packed in every liferaft or grab bag.

Flares – red parachute*

SOLAS specification red parachute flares, with self-container launchers, reach 300 m (1000 ft) in altitude and burn for a minimum of 40 seconds. Pack plenty for any trip to sea; they can attract attention at great distances, including ships that are over your horizon.

Orange smoke flares are the first choice for daylight signalling.

Radar reflector*

This is a SOLAS requirement if an efficient radar transponder (SART) is not included in the liferaft. A raft cannot reflect radar waves but unfortunately it is hard to get a reflector high enough to be effective especially in a big sea. If your emergency pack includes one this is good; if not, seriously consider purchasing a SART instead. If money is very tight a radar reflector is better than nothing.

Rescue line and quoit*

This should be included in every liferaft with not less than 30 m (100 ft) of buoyant line, and fastened to the raft. It is designed to be thrown from the liferaft to a survivor in the water, to assist them reaching the raft.

SART*

A Search and Rescue Transponder, also called a Radar Transponder, is an extremely valuable addition to your EPIRB:

- It returns a magnified, directional, unmistakable, emergency image to any marine radar.
- The signal is received by any marine radar operating within range.
- Most commercial vessels and larger yachts have radar.
- The distinctive signal is easily recognised and much easier to spot than the single echo from a radar reflector.
- It does not require specialized equipment for homing (unlike the 121.5 MHz frequency used by an EPIRB).

21

- The radar can then be used to guide the rescue craft to the exact location of the SART.
- It is required aboard any vessel that is GMDSS compliant.
- It is included in some SOLAS 'A' liferaft packs.

Signal card*

A waterproof copy of the illustrated table of SOLAS No 2 Lifesaving Signals (see inside back cover) should be included in every liferaft. These visual signals are used between shore stations in the UK and ships in distress.

Signal mirror*

Also known as a heliograph, this is the most basic and probably cheapest all-round signalling device for use on land or sea. Its advantages include:

- It is compact and simple to use.
- Any shiny object can be used, including a compact disk.
- A purpose-made mirror is brighter and easier to aim.
- Buoyant waterproof models are designed for marine use. Make sure the instructions for use are on waterproof paper.
- It is used to reflect the sun's rays towards rescue personnel.
- It can be used to transmit Morse code but a simple flash is easier to send.
- In normal sunlight the flash can be seen from at least ten miles.
- A signal mirror will take up little room in your grab bag.
- The more you have the better, pack one for each crewmember.
- With two mirrors you can sweep the horizon.

Strobe light

A rapidly flashing strobe light stands out in open water. It is blindingly bright at close range but further away it is less obvious because the light is dispersed rather than directed. Its major advantage is that it can operate unattended, but the directed light from even a very small flashlight will be visible at a much great distance. Attach a strobe to the outside of the liferaft at night for added visibility, if the raft is not already fitted with one.

Survival craft radio

Special waterproof VHFs are manufactured, as they are required aboard GMDSS compliant vessels. The ultimate grab bag, where money was no object, would include one of these.

Whistle*

A whistle will not attract the attention of a ship or passing aeroplane, but it can help anyone in the water to locate the liferaft. They are cheap and small, so pack a couple of powerful ones. In theory everyone in the liferaft should be carrying one, attached to their lifejacket.

MAINTENANCE AND PROTECTION

The better the quality of your liferaft, the fewer of these items you should need to use. Unfortunately the longer you have to survive in the raft, the more items you will need. An ocean grab bag and liferaft should include at least one of every item here, whereas a yacht never venturing far from shore can reduce this list.

Bailer*

Every liferaft should come with a bailer, though their quality may be doubtful. Sadly your liferaft is unlikely to stay dry and you will be doing a lot of bailing. A plastic dinghy bailer with a handle is cheap enough, so pack a couple. Small items can be packed inside them, so they shouldn't take up too much room. If you have enough space include a hand pump type as well; it will remove large quantities of water quickly and easily.

Bucket

A bucket has many uses from additional bailer to makeshift privy. A collapsible model or a folding bowl will fit inside a grab bag. Otherwise pack a child's seaside bucket. Add the location of the ship's buckets used for washing down etc to your Last Minute Grabs list (see page 39) and use them as carrying containers at abandon ship time.

Chemical heat pack

Hand and body chemical heat packs can provide welcome warmth; the beginnings of hypothermia can set in after a very short time in almost any waters. The hand packs give six hours of gentle warmth, and the body packs 20 hours. The colder the conditions you will be sailing in, the more of these you should include in your grab bag.

Diving mask

If you need to swim under the raft to carry out any repairs you will be very grateful that you packed one of these. It can also be used by the lookout as protection against driving rain or heavy seas.

Inflatable cushions

Some sort of inflatable cushion or mattress will make life very much more comfortable, especially if your liferaft has no additional insulated floor, either inflatable or foam. It will help to keep you above the water that inevitably finds its way into a raft.

Light sticks

Many rafts have no light or, where fitted, it cannot be turned off. Whatever your liferaft has, it will not last long and you will need some other form of interior light at night. Chemical light sticks are cheap to buy and are unaffected by the marine environment, giving a gentle light that can last all night. However they are easy to activate accidentally and must be packed very carefully.

Battery operated waterproof light sticks, sold in dive shops, are much longer lasting and can be switched on and off. But they are vulnerable in the marine environment, like all electrical items.

Pack a selection of chemical and battery operated models for the best of both worlds.

Paddles*

A pair of paddles should be included in every liferaft, to assist with moving away from the mother ship. Not all paddles are full sized or buoyant, one liferaft manufacturer for example supplies hand paddles made of fabric. It is unlikely that you will be paddling far in most liferafts though. Certainly a circular raft is hard to move in a particular direction with paddles alone.

Pump*

A bellows or hand pump should be part of every liferaft equipment bag for topping up the buoyancy chambers, but the quality is often miserable. It should be in one piece, ready for use without any assembling; if yours is not, pack one that is in your grab bag. It is a vital piece of equipment for long time survival in a liferaft; in fact a spare one is a very good idea for an ocean grab bag. An inflatable dingy pump may be an option, used with an adapter, but make sure it isn't designed for foot use only. Check with your liferaft supplier that any pump you choose will work with your raft.

Repair kit*

Liferafts all come with a repair kit of some kind but not necessarily a useful one, so check it carefully. It's all too common to find the kit consists of patches and glue that require a clean and dry surface, almost inconceivable in a liferaft! Make up your own kit, with equipment that is suitable for your liferaft and pack it near the top of your grab bag, with the following:

- Spare canopy and raft material.
- Glue that will work in a wet and salty environment.
- Variety of needles, including sail repair needles, some waxed thread and sewing awl.
- Assorted sized leak stopper plugs for a temporary repair.
- Assorted sized hose clamps to tighten the raft material around a plug.

- Assorted sized raft repair clamps. These are the easiest way to repair a hole with an airtight seal.
- Spare plugs for pressure release and topping up valves.

Rope

Pack a large assortment of long lengths of rope and twine in your grab bag to use as lashings, lanyards and for general improvisation.

Safety knife*

This has a blunt tipped blade supposedly incapable of harming the raft or a person. It is included with the liferaft, stored near the entrance to cut the painter if necessary. A knife meeting SOLAS specifications will have a buoyant handle. This knife is not likely to be much use for any serious cutting and you will need to supplement it – see Knives in the Survival and Morale section.

Sail repair tape

Heavy-duty sail tape is designed for the salt environment and is very useful for quick repairs and improvisations. This makes a valuable addition to the more multipurpose elephant tape included under Miscellaneous.

Sea anchor*

Also called a drogue, it's purpose is to reduce the drift rate of the liferaft and to reduce the risk of capsize. A sea anchor has an additional use, to help the paddles move a circular liferaft in a particular direction. Unfortunately they are all too easy to lose in rough weather.

- Every liferaft needs one, especially boat-shaped rafts.
- A self-deploying version attached to your liferaft is best.
- Include at least one spare in your grab bag, unless you have a SOLAS emergency liferaft pack.
- Ensure there is a minimum of 15 m of attachment line with swivels at each end to help prevent fouling.

Sponges*

Sponges are cheap and included in many liferaft packs. SOLAS packs include two, while the 1998 Sydney–Hobart Race Coroner recommended one per person. In theory they are for drying and mopping up residual water from the floor of the raft. They are also very useful for collecting condensation from the inside of the canopy to drink, so keep at least one free of salt water for this purpose. Very absorbent small sponges, that require only one hand to squeeze out, are best.

Sun screen

Sun screen is an important protection against the misery of sunburn when you are on the water. It is very easy to underestimate the power of the sun, even on an overcast day, to burn a pale skin. This is especially true in the tropics but a bright day in the high latitudes can burn too. Pack high SPF waterproof sunscreen and zinc oxide or special ultra protection cream for the lips and nose, no matter how close to shore you sail.

Thermal protective aid*

A space blanket is not a substitute for a thermal protective aid; it is unsuitable for liferaft use. Instead you should use a thermal protective aid (TPA). This is a special bag designed to fully enclose a person, covering from head to toe and always including a hood.

It keeps a survivor warm by reflecting back the body heat and is a lifesaving piece of kit in the treatment of hypothermia.

Body-shaped models feature arms and legs, allowing various activities without removing the TPA. A bag shape is more efficient at retaining heat and could accommodate two people for rewarming. The outer edges are sealed, except the cuffs of arms and it is impermeable up to the zip or Velcro. Even in a partly water-filled liferaft your feet will remain dry.

This thermal protective aid is a highly visible orange colour. It would be useful to aid the recovery of a casualty overboard.

Make sure you pack one for every crewmember, no matter how little else you pack in your grab bag; ideally include a selection of the two shape types.

Umbrella

This might seem a strange item to include in your grab bag, and those of Italian extraction may consider it very unlucky, but it can be very useful:

- It is light and cheap.
- It can be used by the liferaft lookout as a sunshade or for rain cover.
- If your raft lacks a canopy, include one per person to provide valuable shade.
- It can act as a rainwater catcher.

Watch hat

To give the watch keeper a measure of comfort, pack a hat to protect against sun or cold, depending upon your sailing area. If your liferaft is a basic inshore model, without a canopy, include a hat for every crewmember.

MEDICAL AIDS

The further you are sailing the more of the following items you should add to your grab bag.

Anti-seasickness tablets*

Even if you are one of those lucky people who never suffers from *mal de mer*, you probably will in a liferaft for the following reasons:

- Abandoning ship more often occurs in rough weather than calm conditions.
- A survival craft is very small and generally tightly enclosed.
- Even if you don't feel sick to start with, seeing someone else ill right next to you is very hard on even the strongest stomach.

Seasickness causes the loss of valuable fluids that may be very difficult to replace in a raft, and can lead to serious dehydration. It also makes you more prone to hypothermia and this can eventually kill you.

There are many different anti-seasickness preparations available over the counter. Pack ones that work for you and your crew and view any in your liferaft pack as extra. Include prescription anti-emetic drugs in your first aid kit.

Enema kit

The MCA issue a list of medical supplies that must be carried by various classes of vessels, which is a valuable guide for any yacht planning to make an ocean passage. An enema kit or rectal drip is on this list, to rehydrate when a patient is unable to take liquids orally. It is a valuable piece of equipment for severe seasickness, when the victim is unable to retain anything taken by mouth and dehydration becomes a major problem. This could happen in a liferaft. Another use for an enema kit is for re-hydration if your water supply is unpalatable. However, this is **not** a method of ingesting seawater.

First aid kit

British SOLAS specified liferaft packs must include a Category C first aid kit packed in a sealed re-useable container together with first aid instructions printed on waterproof paper. The Category C medical supplies are listed in the chart on page 29. If your liferaft kit does not include this or its equivalent, consider having a Category C kit packed in your liferaft or included in your grab bag.

Your Last Minute Grabs list should include the yacht's medical kit packed in a waterproof container. In case it is impossible to grab the yacht's kit, particularly the prescription drugs, in time, consider adding a few duplicate items to your grab bag especially when sailing offshore:

- Prescription topical anti-bacterial ointment, as germs breed quickly in a liferaft.
- Aspirin as a first aid treatment for heart attacks.
- Transparent waterproof and breathable adhesive bandages, which if put on dry skin will stay in place and seal a wound even in water.
- Prescription anti-emetic in suppository or injectable form for severe seasickness.
- Inflatable splints for broken limbs.

A comprehensive medical kit is useless without some knowledge and training. At least two members of the crew should know what to do in a medical emergency, and ideally everyone should have a basic knowledge, especially of resuscitation and CPR.

Petroleum jelly

It is not only a valuable medical addition but can also be used for protecting metal. It is an extremely versatile product for lubrication.

Seasickness bags*

It is bad enough being seasick, but having nothing to be sick into makes your misery total. Pack a roll or two of cheap plastic bags in your grab bag; these are much better than the airline style paper bags, which could disintegrate if the liferaft is very wet.

Sunburn cream*

It's hard for fair skinned individuals to avoid getting sunburned, especially in the tropics on deceptive overcast days. Pack at least one tube, more for large crews; creams that include aloe are very good for treating sunburn.

FOOD AND DRINK

Food and water are unnecessary in the short term. If you are sailing inshore in busy waters, carrying an EPIRB and a portable VHF, you probably do not need any of the items in this list. On the other hand if you are planning to sail further afield or you have skimped on the equipment in the Search and Research category then rescue may be delayed. Even with plenty of signalling equipment, when crossing

Liferaft First Aid Kit (Category C Medical Supplies)

Ref No	Statutory treatment	Recommended medicine and dosage	Quantity
1	**Cardio vascular**		
(b)	Anti-angina preparations *For suspected heart attack or heart pain*	Glyceryl trinitrate spray 400 micrograms/metered 200 dose aerosol or transdermal patches 5mg x 2	1 unit
(d)	Anti-haemorrhagics (anti bleeding) (including uterotonics if there are women with potential for child-bearing on board)	i) Phytomenadione (Vitamin K1) 0.2ml (1ampoule) paediatric injection *anti-haemorrhage for newborn babies*	1
		ii) Ergometrine maleate 500mg injection Oxytocin 5 units in 1ml ampoule *For use immediately after delivery of baby or for bleeding after miscarriage*	1
2	**Gastro intestinal system**		
(b)	Anti-emetics (anti-sickness)	Hyoscine hydrobromide 0.3mg tabs	60
(d)	Anti-diarrhoeals	Codeine phosphate 30mg tabs (also painkiller)	20
3	**Analgesics and anti-spasmodics**		
(a)	Analgesics (painkillers)	i) Paracetamol *Mild to moderate pain*	50
		ii) Codeine phosphate (see 2d) *Moderate to severe pain*	Use 2(d)
4	**Nervous system**		
(c)	Seasickness remedies	Hyoscine hydrobromide (see 2b)	Use 2(b)
9	**Medicines for external use**		
(a)	Skin medicine		
	– Antiseptic solutions	100ml solution or pre-impregnated wipes containing 0.015% w/v chlorhexidine and 0.15% w/v cetrimide	1 bottle or 1 pack wipes
	– Burn preparations	Cetrimide cream 50g tube	1

Medical Equipment

Ref No	Statutory treatment requirements	Recommended specification	Quantity
1	**Resuscitation equipment**		
	Mask for mouth to-mouth resuscitation	Laerdal pocket mask	1
2	**Dressing and suturing equipment**		
	Adhesive elastic bandage	Adhesive elastic bandage 7.5cm x 4m	1
	Disposable polyethylene gloves	Large size	5prs
	Adhesive dressings	Assorted, sterile	20
	Sterile compression bandages and unmedicated dressings	Medium, 10 x 8cms	6
		Large, 13 x 9cms	2
		Extra large, 28 x 17.5cms	2
	Adhesive sutures or zinc oxide bandages	75mm adhesive suture strips	6
	Sterile gauze compresses	Packet containing 5 sterile gauze pads size 7.5cms x 7.5cms	1
	Recommended additional items		
	Scissors	Stainless steel or sterile disposable	1 pr
	Calico triangular bandages	About 90 x 127cm	4
	Medium safety pins, rustless		6
	Sterile paraffin gauze dressings		10
	Plastic burn bags		1

The Reference Number refers to the number allocated to the medicine or equipment in MSN 1726

oceans or sailing far off normal shipping routes help may be some time in arriving. In the medium term you will need water and in the long-term food, plus a means of gathering both yourself.

Can opener*

An opener is included in liferaft packs that contain water and food, to open the tins. You and your crew should all be wearing a multipurpose tool or folding knife, making this item unnecessary, but, for security, include at least one can opener in your grab bag to undo any tins you might snatch from the galley.

Containers

Use various sizes of containers with watertight lids, to pack items in your grab bag. The containers can serve double duty as water collectors or bailers. Also include collapsible water carriers to store collected or made water and to hold the water from the liferaft water packs.

Cutlery

For a small amount of money and space, a few sets of camping or plastic picnic cutlery make everyone feel more civilised.

Cutting board

Using a cutting board in the bottom of your grab bag to make it firm and easier to handle was discussed earlier. Though it is possible to improvise using some types of paddles supplied in a liferaft, others such as the canvas style would be hopeless. If you want to fillet a fish, for example, a board is invaluable. A polyethylene antibacterial kitchen chopping board is ideal, as water will not hurt it. If space is at a premium choose a small 'backpackers' chopping board.

Drinking cups*

Liferaft equipment that includes water also includes a graduated drinking cup to divide up the water fairly. Add some plastic picnic style cups, so you can toast each other with a cocktail hour water ration! They can serve double functions as bailers or water catchers.

Drinking water*

SOLAS 'A' liferaft packs contain 1.5 l of water per person, while 0.5 l is common in offshore packs. If you are planning to undertake an ocean passage ensure your liferaft contains at least 0.5 l per person; if this is impossible pack water into your grab bag. In addition, even if you have a portable watermaker, before any long passage fill as many large plastic bottles 80 per cent full of water as you have room for, or empty 20 per cent from large bottles of mineral water and reseal. Store these on deck as near your grab bag or liferaft as possible. Tied together with a floating line, these partially filled bottles will float in seawater and can be towed behind the raft to free up space inside.

Fishing kit*

A fishing kit is included in many offshore liferafts and usually comprises a line and six hooks. No bait is supplied and since fish should not be eaten without a plentiful supply of water (see Chapter 6), the inclusion of fishing gear may be questionable, especially if all you have is the 0.5 l of water supplied in non-SOLAS liferaft packs. So why have fishing equipment? Four good reasons:

- The rescue authorities may have been alerted, but they still have to reach you.
- Long-term survival in a liferaft depends on obtaining food as well as water.
- Fishing helps pass the time and can improve morale.
- The equipment can be put to another use such as repairing the liferaft.

Your grab bag should include a fishing kit with tackle to catch small to medium fish, not large game fish that would be impossible to land safely in a vulnerable liferaft. Unless you are a fishing expert, visit a specialist shop and ask for help in packing a small but comprehensive kit. Make sure everything is of the highest quality and anything metal is, if possible, made from stainless steel to prevent serious rusting as it sits in your grab bag. The kit should include:

- 100 m (300 ft) light fishing line
- Two small hand winders, if they are too big for your bag consider a kite winder
- Wire leaders with clip-on swivels
- Clip-on swivels
- Assorted sinkers
- Plentiful supply of assorted hooks
- Various lures
- Small gaff or net to help land fish
- Waterproof instruction booklet

Food rations*

The 10,000 kJ per person packed in a SOLAS 'A' liferaft pack is approximately three days' food in mild or warm weather. In cold weather and cold waters, where more energy and thus food is required to keep warm, this ration will not last as long. Liferaft survival rations are specially designed for consumption with minimal water and so they are high in carbohydrates, and low in protein (which requires more water for digestion/elimination). Buy this special food to pack in your grab bag, particularly if your liferaft does not include any, or only a small amount. They may not taste great, but they are better than anything else you can buy.

Do not pack the dehydrated food found in outdoor stores for, like the food you are likely to catch, it requires much more water.

Extra ration items should be high in carbohydrate and sugar, low in protein:

- Boiled sweets (hard candy)
- Chocolate
- Dried fruit
- Energy bars
- Glucose tablets
- Tinned fruit
- Tinned sweetened milk

Funnel

Useful to transfer water between containers and ensures not a drop is wasted.

Gloves

A couple of pairs of thick gloves, either leather or man-made material with non-slip palms, are invaluable to protect hands, especially when fishing.

Multivitamin tablets

For long-term liferaft survival include 30 days' supply per person of chewable multivitamin tablets.

Watermaker

A reverse osmosis watermaker is the only reliable way of making drinking water out of salt water, and handheld units are included in some liferafts as part of the standard equipment. With your EPIRBs this is the most important item you can pack in a grab bag. There are, at present, only two choices of small manual watermakers on the market, both made by PUR:

- Survivor 06 – can make just over 1 l ($^1/_4$ gallon) of fresh water per hour.
- Survivor 35 – the bigger version, can make 5.5 l (1.2 gallons) per hour, preferable for crews of eight or more.

Neither is cheap but then nor is your life or that of your crew.

The PUR 06 watermaker is lightweight and easy to use.

SURVIVAL AND MORALE

The items in this category are a mixture of those required to live for a long period in the liferaft and those that may be needed at any time, plus a few items designed to keep everyone entertained.

Charts

Ship routeing, current and wind charts are not so much for navigation, which is very difficult in an inflatable liferaft, but should be included with morale in mind. Used with your compass they will give you an idea of where you are drifting, possible landfalls and sources of rescue. If your charts are not on waterproof paper, laminate them.

Compass

Pack a small plastic compass to keep track of how you are drifting or for use if you reach the shore.

Knife

Include a large sturdy fixed blade knife in your grab bag with a plastic sheath. A dive knife may be suitable, but some survivalists recommend avoiding a double-edged knife. Pack the knife blade covered in plenty of petroleum jelly to prevent rusting as it sits in your grab bag.

Knife sharpener

A stone or ceramic sharpener is best as it will not be adversely affected by salt water.

Land survival book

The Collins Gem SAS Survival Book, for example, is small enough to fit into a corner of your grab bag and yet is very comprehensive. If you make your own way ashore in a desolate part of the world it will be an invaluable guide to living off the land. Pack it inside at least two sealed plastic bags to keep it dry until you reach land.

Land survival kit

Pack a few things for landfall, either a ready-made set or select your own small items. Make sure they are packed in a pocket-sized watertight container and include firelighters, matches, magnifying glass, water purification tablets, a wire saw and a snare.

Lighter

A windproof refillable lighter (with spare butane) will be useful for sealing things like polypropylene rope in the liferaft as well as for starting a fire ashore.

Multipurpose tool

Everyone aboard a yacht should carry his or her own folding knife but also pack into the grab bag at least one multipurpose tool. Choose one with a good assortment of extras such as pliers, bottle opener, scissors, screwdrivers, wire cutter, serrated knife, file, awl/punch etc. Use petroleum jelly to coat the blades etc and if possible vacuum seal the tool to prevent rusting.

Pack of cards

A pack of waterproof playing cards is ideal to while away the hours of waiting.

Pens and pencils

Pack a few writing instruments that work on waterproof paper; you'll need to keep score of that poker game.

Scissors

Include a strong pair of kitchen scissors in your grab bag. These are extremely useful, especially when conditions are too rough to use a knife safely. Pack the scissors with the blades coated in petroleum jelly.

Survival instructions*

Every liferaft should come with some basic instructions about survival. One copy of this book, sealed in a couple of plastic bags, should be packed into your grab bag. Alternatively, remove and laminate the pages you wish to take with you.

Towels

Pack a couple of hand towels, well sealed against water. They can be used in many ways for repairs and improvisations; such as a pad to stop bleeding, protecting against chafe, cleaning, collecting water, as well as the obvious: drying yourself.

Waterproof paper notebook

It is important you keep a log in a liferaft, as a memory aid and for morale. Make sure any paper you pack is waterproof.

PERSONAL

Contact lens kit

If any of the crew wears contact lenses, include the appropriate maintenance kit or some daily wear lenses as appropriate. Make sure you also include a pair of prescription glasses for any contact lens wearer, as it may be impossible to keep wearing the lenses and the crew may not be wearing them when abandoning ship.

Credit card

Duplicate or spare credit cards can ease things when you reach shore, especially in a foreign country. Ensure the credit card is the type that will enable you to get a cash advance from a bank, ATM or cashpoint machine.

Money

Sometimes nothing but cash will do, so include some in your grab bag; how much is up to you. If you are sailing locally only, include the currency of the country in small denominations. Those travelling further afield should include US dollars, which are widely accepted.

Personal hygiene items

Toothbrush, toothpaste and some moist towelettes are a great morale booster, plus helping to keep you healthy. Brushing their teeth makes most people feel much better, especially if they have been seasick. With water at a premium washing is likely to be impossible, but a box of baby wipes or other moist wipes will help clean your skin of salt and reduce the likelihood of salt-water boils. Women will appreciate the inclusion of a few feminine sanitation items.

Personal identification documents

If the yacht is travelling out of your home country make sure you include a photocopy of everyone's passport and other relevant ID in the grab bag. Photocopy the documents onto waterproof paper or laminate ordinary paper. Check, prior to departure, that everyone has another copy of his or her ID kept somewhere ashore.

Prescription eyeglasses

Pack a spare pair of glasses in a rigid case for each crewmember that needs them. Even a not quite current prescription is better than nothing. Include some cheap glasses for the longsighted; they can be very useful for magnifying things.

Personal inspiration

This may be a religious book, a collection of poems, something for meditation or whatever else is appropriate to your beliefs or views. It's a bit like the classic BBC radio programme *Desert Island Discs*, which always allows the castaway to take a book of their choice, though in their case the Bible or other religious work, plus the complete works of Shakespeare, are already on the 'island'. The BBC 'castaway' is also allowed an inanimate luxury item which has no practical value; perhaps you could include something too, though the most popular choice of a piano might be a bit impractical!

Personal medicine

Include a supply of any drugs required by any of the crew in the grab bag, being sure to rotate them regularly. If the required drugs must be kept refrigerated make sure they are stored in as accessible a position as possible in a watertight container, and add it to the Last Minute Grabs list. It's difficult to know exactly how much to pack, especially as lack of food and water can affect the actions of drugs, perhaps 30 days for an ocean grab bag and 5 days for a coastal bag.

Spare clothing

Everyone should be wearing as many layers of clothing as possible before taking to the liferaft, but in a very rapid exit some people might not have time to dress warmly. Extra clothes packed in a watertight bag are a bonus, especially if it is necessary to enter the water. A vacuum-bagging machine can reduce a large woollen sweater or fleece to a very small size and ensure it stays completely dry.

Sunglasses

A pair of sunglasses for each crewmember need not cost a lot, but will be very welcome if it's warm and sunny. One pair for the watchkeeper is vital.

Yacht's papers

Include a copy of the yacht's registration and any other official documents, photo-copied onto waterproof paper or you can laminate ordinary paper. Make sure you keep another copy of everything ashore, including insurance documents, and consider filing a second set with the holder of your Voyage Details Plan (see Appendix 1).

MISCELLANEOUS

These items do not fit anywhere else or, like elephant tape, they overlap several categories.

Batteries

Including spare alkaline batteries for all electrical equipment has been mentioned with individual items, but it is reiterated here as a reminder. Make sure you rotate these batteries regularly with the yacht's supply.

Camera

If you have a little spare room pack a disposable waterproof camera in your grab bag, so you can show your friends what happened in the liferaft.

Contents list

As well as marking everything inside your grab bag in waterproof ink you need to include a complete contents list. Detail everything inside your grab bag and print the list on waterproof paper or laminate it.

Include brief instructions on how to use and maintain each item where appropriate. Place the list at the top of the grab bag and place a second copy in the onboard Training Manual. Place a third copy in the Maintenance Record Book with expiry dates of all items. Leave copies with your designated shoreside contacts, so rescuers understand you have the potential to survive a long time.

Do not forget to update the contents list whenever you make any changes to the grab bag.

Elephant tape

This is commonly known in the USA as 'duct tape' and books have been written in honour of its many uses. Get the very best quality tape you can find, two rolls at least, as you will want one for the yacht if you don't already have it aboard. Test that the type you choose will stick in the wet as some brands are better than others. You can use this tape for all sorts of repairs and improvisations such as:
* Liferaft leaks above the waterline.
* Securing a bandage or splint to a patient.
* Covering the strobe light on an EPIRB.
* Taping containers to obtain a completely watertight seal.

Foil

A large sheet of thick aluminium foil, folded up, takes little room and has many uses, including radar reflection and fishing lures.

Plastic bags

It would be difficult to pack too many plastic bags. They may be environmentally unfriendly but they will be invaluable in your liferaft. Include a selection from huge to tiny together with plenty of assorted sized, resealable, heavy weight, freezer bags (the zipper style are particularly easy to use).

LAST MINUTE GRABS

Some of the things in the other categories may also belong here on your boat, as they or additional units are going to be stored outside your grab bag. Your Last Minute Grabs list should be pinned up in a prominent position aboard your yacht. Create a list to ensure you do not forget something essential when you abandon ship. See page 39 for an example of one such list.

Binoculars

You could pack a spare pair in your grab bag, but it is more likely that you will take those from the yacht. They will help you make sure you are seeing a genuine rescue craft before you set off a flare.

Cellular telephone

While a cellular mobile phone should not be your only means of making a call for help, it may be a valuable additional method of making contact when you are in a liferaft and close to the shore. Make sure you have a waterproof case to protect it.

Cockpit cushions

These can add to comfort and warmth in the liferaft, especially if it lacks an insulated floor. Buoyant cushions such as the US Type IV personal flotation device can also be used to help survivors in the water.

EPIRB

Collect the Class I EPIRB from its hydrostatic holder or any other EPIRB stored outside the grab bag. The more EPIRBs you have in your liferaft the better.

Extra food and drink

Grab as much as you can from the galley, especially the cookie jar and other carbohydrates. Add as many soft drinks and cartons of long life milk as you can, and do not forget any large water containers you have stored on deck. If there is time fill every possible container with drinking water. Leave the alcohol behind; it can wait for the survival celebration once you are safely ashore.

Fleece blankets

Many small yachts use fleece blankets as bedding and these are ideal for extra warmth in a liferaft even if they are slightly damp.

Heavy weather gear

Even if you are in the tropics, make sure everyone has put on their waterproofs on

Sample 'Last Minute Grabs' List

Equipment	Location
EPIRB	Aft deck in float free holder
Buckets	Aft deck locker
Man overboard buoy	Aft deck, port side
Extra water	Cockpit table
Pyrotechnic container	Cockpit
Cockpit cushions	Cockpit
Spear gun	Rack behind cockpit
Portable VHFs (2)	On charge in workshop
Medical kit	Skipper's cabin
Fleece blankets	Individual cabins
Lifejackets	Individual cabins
Spare warm clothing	Individual cabins
Cellular phones	Individual cabins
Heavy weather gear	Wet gear locker
Binoculars	Chart table
Portable GPS	Chart table
Sextant & tables	Chart table
Radio	Main saloon, starboard aft locker
Extra food & drink	
Cookie jar, fruit, chocolate, breakfast cereals	Galley
Long life milk and soft drinks	Under floor, aft saloon
Tinned food, dried fruit	Starboard seating in main saloon
Plus any other food to hand	
John's prescription drugs	Galley fridge, top shelf

top of layers of clothing, before leaving the yacht. It can be cold at night. The higher your latitude and colder the water the more you should put on to protect yourself from hypothermia.

Immersion suit

In cold waters – those less than 21ºC (70ºF) – an immersion or survival suit is highly recommended. Remember that some immersion suits are not insulated and it is essential that warm clothing be worn before putting on the suit. In theory survival suits should be in the grab bag, but they are often large and each can usually be considered as a separate stand-alone grab bag.

Lifejacket

Without a lifejacket even an Olympic champion swimmer will have difficulty in staying afloat in cold water because of the disabling effects of cold, shock and cramp. A lifejacket:

- will keep you afloat without effort or swimming, regardless of how much clothing you are wearing;
- must be of sufficient buoyancy for your possible sailing conditions;
- should be carried for everyone aboard your yacht, including any children;
- must be worn if abandoning ship is a possibility, in case you end up in the water;
- can serve as a cushion to sit on inside the liferaft.

Man overboard buoy

This can be used for its original purpose, to attract attention, but also to jury rig a mast or to hold up a radar reflector or SART.

Medical kit

Ideally this will be in a waterproof and sealed container, which will make its transfer to the liferaft easy. If the medical kit is packed in something less impermeable to water consider purchasing a better box, before you sail. The sea is a damp environment even aboard a large yacht and medical equipment can be spoiled very quickly. Remember to take the prescription drugs container, if that is stored in a different location.

Portable VHF

A survival craft radio is included in the Search and Rescue category but even if your grab bag includes one, you should still take any other portable VHFs to the liferaft. The ideal VHF should be:

- waterproof and preferably submersible;
- fitted with a lithium ion battery, the expensive sort that can be recharged at any time without waiting for the battery to run down;

An ICOM hand-held VHF radio which is fully waterproof, has a large illuminated display and powered by a lithium battery.

- kept fully charged;
- able to use alkaline batteries, with spares stored in your grab bag.

If your handheld VHF is not waterproof make sure to include a special watertight bag.

Portable GPS

Most yachts now carry at least one handheld GPS and celestial navigation is fast becoming a dying art. Knowing where exactly you are in a liferaft is nice, even if you cannot influence where you are going. Make sure your model is waterproof or kept in a waterproof case.

Radio

Many yachts, especially those cruising, have a short wave portable radio on board to listen to commercial stations. Packed in a waterproof bag this can provide morale boosting entertainment in a liferaft. Don't forget to include the correct spare batteries in the grab bag.

Satellite mobile telephone

In the future a satellite phone will be as common and may even be as cheap as a cellular phone is today. When that time comes the items we will all need inside a grab bag are likely to be few, even for an ocean crossing.

Sextant and tables

If your survival craft is an inflatable liferaft you are unlikely to be able to sail it effectively. In those circumstances traditional navigation equipment taken from your yacht is unlikely to be of much use except as a morale boosting item or a chance to pass on your knowledge to a captive audience. If sailing is a real possibility then your sextant will be very useful, along with a good compass, time-piece, tables, charting tools, charts and anything else you require to make a fix.

Spare clothing

If there are no, or very few, spare clothes packed in the grab bag make sure they are on your Last Minute Grabs list.

Spear gun

Those who fish at sea for food and not for fun often keep a spear gun aboard. Whilst its main function is usually below water, it is an excellent method of killing a large fish caught when trawling, as well as providing an extra line to help bring it aboard. A spear gun used above water must be powered by bands rather than compressed air, which is only suitable for underwater use. If you carry a spear gun, include it in your Last Minute Grabs, as it can be used to catch the fish attracted to your liferaft. Make sure your grab bag is one of the places you store spare bands, shafts and tips.

SHOPPING LISTS

To help you decide how much or how little to include in your grab bag, suggested shopping lists for different voyages and locations are shown on the following pages.

The Ocean Grab Bag

The ultimate bag for round the world cruising and ocean passage making. It includes everything detailed in this chapter.

The Coastal Grab Bag

This assumes all passages are close to shore where rescue will be measured in hours, or at worst a day or so in less populated areas. This grab bag could also be used for short passages further offshore, especially with the addition of some water.

Warm Water Variation

Ideal for those sailing in tropical waters, where the risk of hypothermia is low.

The Cold Weather Variation

This version is for sailors living in a temperate or colder climate, especially those who sail in the winter season.

The Minimalist Grab Bag

This list is for those with the best liferaft money can buy and the appropriate GMDSS equipment for their sailing area. It assumes you can send an automated distress message using the on-board DSC radio and satellite communications equipment. Wherever you are in the world help should arrive soon, but just in case it is delayed for any reason a watermaker is included. Meanwhile with your portable satellite phone you can use your time in the raft to sell your survival story to the media!

Ocean Grab Bag List

Search & Rescue
EPIRB x 2
Flares – buoyant orange smoke x 2
Flares – red handheld x 6
Flares – red parachute x 6
Flashlight x 3
Kite – parafoil
Radar reflector
Rescue line & quoit
SART
Signal card
Signalling mirror 1pp
Strobe light
Survival craft radio
Whistle x 2

Maintenance & Protection
Bailer x 2
Bucket
Chemical heat pack 2pp
Diving mask
Inflatable cushions
Light sticks x 8
Paddles
Pump x 2
Repair kit
Rope
Safety knife
Sail repair tape
Sea anchor x 3
Sponges 1pp
Sunscreen
TPA 1pp
Umbrella
Watch hat

Personal
Contact lens kit
Credit card
Money
Personal hygiene supplies
Personal ID
Prescription eyeglasses
Personal inspiration
Personal medicine
Spare clothing
Sunglasses
Yacht's papers

Medical
Anti-seasickness tablets 6pp +
Enema kit
First aid kit
Petroleum jelly
Seasickness bags
Sunburn cream

Food & Drink
Can opener x 2
Containers, assorted
Cutlery 1pp
Cutting board
Drinking cup 1pp
Drinking water 1.5 litres pp
Fishing kit
Food rations
Funnel
Gloves
Multivitamin tablets 30pp
Watermaker

Survival & Morale
Charts
Compass
Knife
Knife sharpener
Land survival book
Land survival kit
Lighter
Multipurpose tool
Pack of cards
Pens & pencils x4
Scissors
Survival instructions
Towels x 2
Waterproof paper and pad x 2

Miscellaneous
Batteries
Camera
Contents list
Elephant tape
Foil
Plastic bags

Note: Delete from this list any items already packed inside your liferaft, if known to be of excellent quality

Coastal Grab Bag List

Search & Rescue
EPIRB x 1
Flare – orange smoke x 1
Flares – red handheld x 3
Flares – red parachute x 3
Flashlight x 2
Kite – parafoil
Portable VHF
Radar reflector
Rescue line & quoit
SART
Signal card
Signalling mirror x 2
Strobe light
Whistle x 2

Food and Drink
Containers, assorted

Survival & Morale
Compass
Knife
Knife sharpener
Land survival book
Land survival kit
Lighter
Multipurpose tool
Pens & pencils x 2
Scissors
Survival instructions
Waterproof paper

Maintenance & Protection
Bailer
Chemical heat pack 1pp
Light sticks x 2
Paddles
Pump
Repair kit
Rope
Safety knife
Sea anchor x 2
Sponges x 2
Sun screen
TPA 1pp
Watch hat

Medical
Anti-seasickness tablets
First aid kit
Seasickness bags

Personal
Credit card
Money
Prescription medicine
Sunglasses
Yacht's papers

Miscellaneous
Batteries
Camera
Contents list
Elephant tape
Plastic bags

Note: Delete from this list any items already packed inside your liferaft, if known to be of excellent quality

Climatic Variations to your Grab Bag

Cold Weather Variation
Add:
- Warm hats
- Gloves
- Extra chemical heat packs
- Extra food
- Additional spare clothes
- Immersion suits

Delete (except in the polar regions):
- Sunglasses
- Sunscreen
- Sunburn cream

Warm Water Variations
Add:
- Sunhats
- Extra sunscreen
- Extra sunburn cream
- Extra water
- Sunglasses 1pp

Delete:
- Chemical heat packs
- Inflatable cushions

Minimalist's Grab Bag List

406 MHz EPIRB with GPS
Inmarsat E EPIRB
Manual watermaker
Portable satellite phone
Immersion suit 1pp

MAINTENANCE AND SERVICE

A grab bag is not a 'buy and forget about it' item of safety equipment; like a liferaft it also needs regular maintenance and money outlay to keep it in perfect condition. When your liferaft is away having its annual service you should unpack your grab bag and check all the items too. Any electronic items should be checked even more often.

For all safety equipment you should:
- Read any owner's manual.
- File a copy of all instructions and information in the crew training manual.
- Add it to the safety equipment list, which should be displayed in a prominent position.
- Enter the item in your Maintenance Record or Log Book, including where appropriate:
  - an inspections checklist
  - maintenance and repair instructions
  - maintenance schedule
  - lubrication points diagram plus recommended lubricants
  - a list of replaceable parts
  - a list of sources of spare parts
  - a record of inspection and maintenance.
- Fill in and send off any registration card.
- Mount or stow the item in its correct position immediately.
- If appropriate practise using the item.

Your EPIRB

To guarantee your EPIRB has every chance of operating correctly if an emergency occurs you should for each beacon:

- Ensure you and your crew know exactly how it works.
- Register it and update the information as necessary.
- Ensure it is stored or secured so that it cannot be accidentally switched on. This is the main cause of expensive time-wasting false alerts.
- Once a week visually inspect for signs of damage or corrosion.
- Once a month and before any long passages, activate the self-test.
- At the start of a season and before any long passage check the battery and any hydrostatic release. Change them if the expiry date is close.

4

ABANDONING SHIP

Collision, fire, flooding and grounding are four of the possible reasons why the skipper of any vessel may have to utter those two words that every sailor dreads: 'Abandon Ship'. This chapter discusses what to do from the moment the skipper gives that order to prepare to abandon ship, until such time as everyone is safely on board the liferaft.

Whether you sail alone or with a large crew, you should have at least given some thought as to how to cope with a disaster and, at best, performed regular practise drills of likely scenarios. In an emergency the human brain falls back on well-learned patterns of behaviour. This is good news for trained crew, but can have unfortunate consequences for untrained people who may react with inappropriate behaviour. Inside the front cover is an Emergency Flowchart for an abandon ship situation; it can be used for practise and real situations. Remember it is always better to remain with your boat:

- A boat is bigger than any liferaft she carries.
- It can better withstand the sea and provide shelter for people.
- It is more easily detectable by the SAR units.
- Crew taking to a liferaft have been lost, whilst the deserted vessel remained afloat.

In some situations, for example an out of control fire, it may be prudent to take to the liferafts and may later be possible to return to the mother ship.

EMERGENCY SIGNALS

It is vitally important that in an emergency you can quickly gather all the crew together. Even on a small boat, someone shouting from the wheel when the engine is running is unlikely to be heard by any crew below. It is important to consider an alternative method of summoning everyone, for example a hand-held foghorn or whistle.

An urgent situation

When an emergency arises the skipper must take charge. Ideally, the skipper will be in control and organising matters rather than actually doing the work. With a small crew the skipper will not have that luxury, but he must:

- Delegate as much as possible.
- Keep an overall picture of the situation.
- Be ready to take immediate action to maintain the safety of life.

The skipper should be guided at all times by his primary responsibilities:
- The safety of those entrusted to his care.
- The safety of the boat.
- The protection of the marine environment.
All other considerations are secondary to these.

Trying to cure the problem must take a very high priority, but an early and immediate attempt should be made to contact other people, such as rescue services and nearby vessels, to alert them to the situation and request assistance. A vessel or crew with a serious problem, but not yet in a distress situation, should send a Pan Pan message rather than a Mayday by radiotelephone

A Pan Pan can be sent with a VHF fitted with a DSC controller by selecting All Ship Calls, then Urgency. Once the alert is sent, the radio will automatically switch to Channel 16, ready for the verbal message. It is important that the Pan Pan includes the position of the yacht as this is not transmitted in an automatic Urgency call.

PREPARING TO ABANDON SHIP

If it is clear that the accident or emergency situation is not going to be resolved, or that there is even a slight possibility that the situation may escalate and become out of control, the skipper must prepare to abandon ship. In the best of all worlds, with a large crew, the various jobs can be carried out while a part of the crew continues to try to save the yacht. With a small crew it may be necessary to cease attempting to cure the problem and get on with preparing to leave the yacht.

Avoiding hypothermia and drowning

The two major threats for people abandoning ship are hypothermia and drowning. **COLD**, not lack of food and water, is the greatest killer after abandoning ship. People become too cold to help themselves in the water, and drown. After boarding a survival craft, even if crew never entered the water and became wet, they can still die of cold if the necessary precautions have not been taken. The epic survival voyages which have attracted publicity in the past have nearly all taken place in tropical waters.

If it should be necessary to enter the water on abandoning the yacht, the initial 'cold shock' may prove disabling or even fatal. Extra clothing will prolong your survival time by reducing loss of body heat. Everyone must:

- Put on extra layers of clothing (wool and polypropylene).
- Put on foul weather gear, fastening tightly at the wrist and ankles (with elephant tape if necessary).
- Add socks, shoes, gloves, hat etc.
- Best of all, wear an immersion suit.
- Finally, add your lifejacket.

Lots of clothes will not weigh you down – in fact the opposite is true. When you enter the water the air trapped between the extra layers of clothing will help your lifejacket keep you afloat. Even if you board the survival craft without getting wet the extra clothing will help to save your life while awaiting rescue. If possible pack spare clothes in a dry bag in case you have to swim; this bag can also be used as a substitute flotation device.

With a lifejacket and ordinary clothes in summer with a UK sea temperature of between 14° and 18°C (57°F and 64°F) you will probably survive between 2 and 9 hours, depending upon whether you are lightly or heavily clad. In a UK winter the seawater temperature is about 7°C (45°F) and the likely survival time is much reduced:

Lightly clad	40 minutes
Heavily clad	80 minutes
Immersion suit	6 to 8 hours

Preparing the liferaft

There are too many stories of crews launching a liferaft and tying it alongside to await orders, only to have it swept away before anyone boarded. During the disastrous 1998 Sydney–Hobart Race the yacht *Naiad* inflated her two liferafts and tethered them to the yacht on the leeward side. A large wave struck the *Naiad* and the liferafts quickly vanished. Liferafts have pockets on the bottom that are designed to fill quickly with water and restrain the liferaft from moving freely through the water. When tied to a moving yacht the liferaft will naturally resist being pulled through the water. Immense strain is placed upon the tether or its anchor point, and one of these will eventually fail.

The liferaft must not be launched until such time as the abandon ship order is given by the skipper, but it must be made ready. Depending upon where a liferaft is stowed normally:

- Release the securing arrangements.
- Move the raft to the launch position:

- the lowest deck
- amidships on the leeward side
- the stern in a calm sea if the boat has a swimming platform.
- Do not inflate the raft on deck:
  - the exploding canister can cause injuries
  - the raft could get jammed
  - parts of the yacht could pierce the raft.
- Make the painter fast to a strong point such as a mooring cleat but definitely not to the lifelines, which could easily break under the strain.

If time permits launch any dinghies, surfboards, canoes or anything else that floats and tie them alongside ready to use or later attach to the liferaft.

Assembling the survival kit

This is where the Last Minute Grabs list (see page 39) is invaluable as a memory aid. Use it while collecting various articles such as binoculars, EPIRB, food and water, medical kit, portable VHF etc. Make sure every item has a long lanyard attached to it. Try to collect everything together with the grab bag, ready to transfer to the liferaft.

If time permits, delegate one person to hand out anti-seasickness tablets with water or a soft drink. A liferaft can affect the strongest stomach and most medicine is only effective before seasickness sets in. Encourage everyone to drink as much water as possible before leaving the yacht, as this will increase the level of body fluids and will also help overcome the possibility of urine retention due to 'mental blockage' later when in the very public confines of a crowded raft.

SUMMONING HELP

Once it becomes obvious that the yacht cannot be saved, assistance must be summoned. A visual representation of the most widely recognised distress signals is shown on the inside back cover.

If possible use VHF, HF, MF, or Inmarsat communication equipment to make the initial distress alert as it allows a direct exchange of information between casualty and rescuer. If a Pan Pan message was sent, upgrade it to a Mayday. Appendices 2 and 3 give examples of Mayday procedure for VHF and SSB to help you create your own cards:

- Include details of your boat and equipment use.
- Place them prominently near your radio equipment.
- Check a novice could use them.
- Use the internationally recognised Mayday format as it ensures all the important information is transmitted; the recipients understand what they hear even if English is their second language.

GMDSS is fully implemented on commercial vessels over 300 GT, and an increasing number of other vessels. These vessels are no longer obliged to listen out on Channel 16 or 2182 MHz. Coastal stations will continue to listen on the designated emergency channels, but in a busy traffic area a poor signal may be lost amongst the background noise. It is highly recommended that all boats have GMDSS compliant equipment with a DSC controller, to attract attention when making a Mayday call. GMDSS is essential for any offshore yacht.

When contact has been made by radio or Inmarsat do not cause confusion by also activating your EPIRB, unless:

- Contact is lost.
- You are told to do so by the rescue authority.
- The radio ceases to work due to total electrical failure, demasting etc.

If a radiotelephone distress message is impossible:

- Use any of the recognised Distress Signals (inside back cover) to attract attention.
- Even if no vessel is in sight consider firing two parachute flares:
  - the first flare to catch someone's eye;
  - the second, three minutes later, to give them a direction
  - do not waste any more until you know help is nearby.
- Close to shore try your cellular mobile telephone:
  - in the UK dial 999 and ask for the Coastguard
  - in the USA call 911 or call the Coast Guard directly.

STAYING WITH THE YACHT

Whilst this book is about abandoning ship, it does not mean you should always take to your liferaft. Your liferaft is the final ultimate retreat; it is NOT the first choice when things go wrong. **Never abandon ship until the last possible moment.** Remember:

- Your yacht is bigger and safer than your liferaft.
- Help may arrive to fight a fire or bring a pump to deal with flooding.
- You may be able to transfer to another vessel or helicopter without ever inflating your raft or getting your feet wet.

ABANDONING THE YACHT

The skipper is the only person who should give the abandon ship order. No matter how large the boat this command must only be issued by word of mouth, to prevent any possibility of confusion.

Once the abandon ship order is given but before the liferaft is actually launched, the skipper should:
- Ensure the engine(s) and propeller(s) are stopped.
- Take a note of the position of the yacht to take to the liferaft.
- Make a final Mayday call to announce the abandonment.
- Check everyone aboard is gathered together dressed in warm clothes or immersion suits.
- Lifejackets are correctly fitted and tightly tied.

Yachts have been reboarded after being abandoned following fire etc. Therefore, time permitting and where appropriate:
- Shut all watertight compartments.
- Close all fuel valves.

Launching the liferaft

Once the order is given to abandon ship, the liferaft must be launched.

1. Check the painter is secured to a strong point.
2. Check that all deck fastenings are undone.
3. Check the water in the launching area is clear of people or obstructions.
4. Throw the raft over the side.
5. Allow the painter to run out to its full extent – this may be any length, SOLAS recommends 15 m (50 ft).
6. Jerk the painter to fire the CO_2 bottle and inflate the liferaft. If the liferaft inflates inverted, take the action given on page 57 to right it.
7. Keep the raft alongside if possible. Hauling in a raft on a long painter is very difficult.
8. Protect the raft from chafing on the side of the yacht and damaging the fabric.

Boarding the liferaft from the yacht

Unloaded liferafts tip over easily, especially before the ballast bags are full of seawater. It is important to get someone heavy aboard as soon as the raft is fully inflated and before any excess gas starts to vent from the overflow valves. Boarding the liferaft without entering the water is the priority to avoid hypothermia or drowning.

Once the first person is aboard the raft, the order in which you transfer everyone else, plus the grab bag, Last Minute Grabs etc, will depend on circumstances and crew numbers.

Actions to take:
- Leave injured survivors until last – other crew may land on them and make the injuries worse.
- Climb aboard using a ladder or rope, if stepping down is impossible. Do not jump onto the liferaft – this could harm you, the raft canopy or other people already inside.
- Tie lanyards, attached to all equipment, to the yacht or liferaft before passing the item from boat to raft.
- Tie water containers (80 per cent full) onto the outside of the raft to float.
- Attach dinghies, canoes or other floating water toys to the raft.

Entering the water from the yacht

If there is no time, or for some other reason it is impossible to bring the liferaft along-side the yacht, you must enter the water. Even in the event of a rapid sinking, you must try to find time to put on a lifejacket and warm clothing or an immersion suit.

When choosing how to leave the yacht bear in mind:
- Drift of the yacht – if conditions allow, leave on the windward side. A yacht stopped and drifting will make more leeway than you, and swimmers could become trapped by the leeward drift of the vessel.
- Position of any survival craft in the water – remember that the survival craft may drift much more quickly than you can swim.
- Without a survival craft in the water, the stern or bow may be the best choice to get clear of the yacht with more certainty.
- The sea state.
- Other hazards, eg burning oil.

Entering the water from a height

Do not jump into the water unless it is essential as sudden immersion in cold water can kill or incapacitate. Use something to lower yourself such as a ladder, a rope or even a hose. Slowly entering the water makes the temperature change more gradual.

If you do have to jump:
- Never jump from more than 6 m (20 ft) wearing an inflated or permanent buoyancy lifejacket.
- Keep your lifejacket on and securely tied.
- Use one hand to hold down the jacket, to stop it hitting your chin on entering the water.

- Always use your other hand to block off your nose and mouth to keep out the water.
- Keep feet together with legs slightly bent.
- Check below to avoid obstructions.
- Jump feet first, looking straight ahead, looking down can make you tumble forward.

ACTION ONCE IN THE WATER

Never remain longer in the water than necessary. Get clear of the boat and into a liferaft as quickly as possible.

Remember that:
- body heat is lost 20 times faster in water than on land
- suction from the yacht sinking is a danger
- there could be an underwater explosion, so get onto any wreckage if you can or swim on your back.

Never swim aimlessly since exercise increases heat loss as the blood supply to the muscles is increased, and warmed water trapped by any clothing is forced out. Float using the HELP (Heat Escape Lessening Posture) position to minimise heat loss:
- Cross your arms and grip the neck of your lifejacket.
- Cross your ankles and draw your knees up to your chest.

In rough seas float with your back to the wind and sea to reduce wave splashes. Use the whistle and light attached to the lifejacket to attract others. Use the loop on the back of the lifejacket to tow an injured person.

Unite with other survivors and huddle to increase your visibility and warmth:
- Form a circle facing inwards.
- Loop arms through each other's lifejackets.
- Intertwine legs to reduce heat loss.

You could use the **crocodile** position, joining in a straight line to:
- Face same direction.
- Maintain contact when swimming towards a liferaft for example.

If you are not wearing a lifejacket float on your back to save energy. Grab anything that might help you float and look out for items that may resurface.

Air trapped in your clothing will provide considerable flotation. Retain boots and shoes, if possible, for future protection.

In cold water:
- **Do not** remove any clothes.
- **Do not** use the 'drown-proofing technique' (putting your head into the water); you cool 80 per cent faster than with your head out of the water.

In warmer water clothing can make a temporary float. For example:
- Tie knots in the legs
- Swing through the air by the waistband to trap the air
- Repeat as air is lost.

Oil fire on the water

If you are in oil-covered water that is free of fire, hold your head high to keep oil out of your eyes.

If the oil is burning:
- Paddle or swim against the wind.
- Discard your lifejacket and swim under the water as far as you can.
- When resurfacing to breathe, make a sweeping movement with your hands to force your body clear and cover your eyes, nose and mouth.
- Sweep the flames clear with broad arm movements across the surface, take a deep breath and get underwater again rapidly.
- Swim clear of the area.

Sharks

Fortunately very few species of sharks attack man without provocation. It is believed that they are very curious and attracted by unusual noise. The highest risk of a shark encounter is when the yacht sinks.

If sharks are in the water with you:
- Get out of the water into the liferaft or onto anything else floating.
- Retain all clothing, especially on the legs and feet, as feet and unclothed areas are attacked first.
- Keep still: move only to keep the shark in sight.
- If swimming is necessary move with rhythmic strokes.
- In a group, form a circle facing outwards.
- Bind bleeding wounds.
- Avoid urinating. If essential void small amounts at long intervals.

- Throw vomit as far away as possible; the same with defaecation.
- Get into an oil patch.
- If attack is imminent, splash and yell but conserve your strength to fight.
- If attacked, kick and strike the shark, going for the gills and eyes.

Boarding a liferaft from the water

Once you reach the liferaft:
- Put your arm through the grablines – hands quickly numb in cold conditions.
- Use any foot and handholds to help you enter the raft.
- If wearing a lifejacket submerge yourself to help 'bob up' higher.
- Assist any weak or injured into the liferaft:
  1 Turn the survivor so that their back is against the liferaft.
  2 Those in the liferaft should then grip him under the arms and on top of the shoulders.
  3 'Dunk' him several times before lifting him in.
  4 The people in the water can help keep the person upright and push up as he is lifted aboard it.

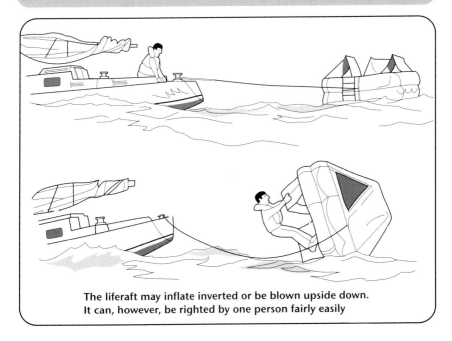

The liferaft may inflate inverted or be blown upside down.
It can, however, be righted by one person fairly easily

RIGHTING A CAPSIZED RAFT

A liferaft may inflate in the inverted position, or be capsized by the winds and waves especially if it is empty. Try to right a capsized raft without entering the water, but beware of any potential hazards that could harm the raft. If necessary, move the liferaft into clear water before attempting to right it. One person can easily right a capsized liferaft, even a very large one, from the water.

To right a liferaft:
- Position the raft with the gas bottle at the downwind side.
- Climb onto the raft from a position close to the gas bottle.
- Standing on the gas bottle, grip the righting strap firmly, then stand upright.
- Check the raft is tilted into the wind.
- Lean back and use your body weight to pull the liferaft over.
- As the liferaft falls backwards exit on your back in a right-hand direction.
- If the raft comes over on top of you, do not worry. Simply back-stroke out from underneath.

Warning: Do not attempt to clear the underside of the liferaft by a forward movement. This will bring you up against the gas bottle and the buoyancy of your life-jacket could trap you. Beware of the stability pockets, they may contain lead weights.

A fully manned liferaft is unlikely to capsize, provided that the drogue is streamed at an early stage and that the occupants sit with their backs against the sides of the liferaft. If capsize does occur carry out the capsize drill as above. **Do not panic.** The raft will float high in the water and air will be trapped inside. Evacuate the liferaft in an orderly manner.

5

Simply boarding a liferaft, especially in rough seas and cold weather, is no guarantee that you will survive. To ensure everyone in a liferaft has some basic information on what to do next, official guidance notes for survival instructions have been included in SOLAS standard liferafts. This chapter expands on these guidance notes with the official wording printed in *bold italic*. The information detailing immediate action in a liferaft is given below. A copy should be made and included:

- at the top of every grab bag, laminated or on waterproof paper.
- in any onboard training manual.

The value of training cannot be over emphasised; it will make a real abandon ship situation much less traumatic and give everyone a much better chance of a successful outcome.

> *SOLAS Instructions for Immediate Action in the liferaft*
> *1 **CUT** painter and get clear of ship.*
> *2 **LOOK** for and pick up other survivors.*
> *3 Ensure sea anchor **STREAMED** when clear of ship.*
> *4 **CLOSE** up entrances.*
> *5 **READ** survival instructions.*

IMMEDIATE ACTIONS IN A LIFERAFT

Certain vital actions must be taken as soon as possible after boarding the liferaft:

CUT the painter and get clear of ship

You are in the liferaft because your boat is sinking or burning out of control. You do not want your new home to be hurt by your old one. You must sever your last tie to the mother ship. A safety knife is stowed near each liferaft entrance to cut the painter.

- Cut the painter as far from the raft as possible, the rope may be useful later.
- Pull in the sea anchor if it streamed automatically when the raft inflated.
- Manoeuvre away using the oars or paddles.
- Use the sea anchor to move the raft, by throwing the sea anchor in the direction you want to go, and heaving on the hawser to pull the raft towards the sea anchor.

LOOK for and pick up other survivors

Once the raft is clear of the sides of the yacht, check for any more survivors in the water. Establish who, if anyone, is missing. Look for lifejacket lights, and listen for whistles or shouts.

With conscious swimmers use the rescue quoit:

- Hold or tie the end of the line in the raft.
- Throw the quoit with its buoyant line to the person in the water.
- Instruct the survivor to put their arm through the quoit, if possible.
- Pull the survivor to the raft.

With an unconscious survivor or someone unable to hold the quoit, it may be necessary to put someone in the water to help. Do not enter the water without a lifejacket. Take the quoit, leaving the end tied to the raft or held by those aboard. Never underestimate the strength of a panic-stricken person in the water, so always approach a survivor from behind. Use the loop on the back of the lifejacket to tow the survivor. Instruct those in the liferaft to pull in both yourself and the survivor. Lift exhausted survivors aboard in the horizontal position, to reduce the chance of a sudden drop in blood pressure.

Ensure sea anchor is STREAMED when clear of the ship

Stream the sea anchor or drogue as soon as possible to:

- Stabilise the raft.
- Reduce the drift away from survivors who may still be in the water.
- Remain near the last position of the yacht, the likely area of maximum search.
- Reduce the risk of capsize.

Adjust the sea anchor so that when the raft is on a wave crest, the drogue is in the wave trough.

CLOSE the raft entrance

In cold weather the body heat of occupants will rapidly warm the interior so close entrances when any inflation relief valve has stopped venting. Tie doorway tapes using slipknots to facilitate untying in a hurry.

In tropical climates, leave entrances open to reduce fluid loss caused by perspiration.

READ survival instructions

Everyone aboard the liferaft should, as soon as possible, read all instructions, including this book.

SECONDARY ACTIONS IN A LIFERAFT

Once the Immediate Actions have been completed, the following secondary actions should be taken as soon as possible. The order in which they are listed here is not necessarily the order in which they should be done; this will depend on the particular circumstances of the situation at the time.

Identify person in charge of liferaft

The skipper from the yacht should be in charge in the liferaft. If he is missing or disabled, either physically or psychologically, a new leader will have to be selected as soon as possible. Choose someone with a strong will to survive for the good of everyone aboard, and assist them by obeying their orders at once. During the first few hours in the liferaft survivors will begin to realise what has happened and the danger, injury and possible death that now surrounds them. The skipper must:

- Provide leadership and assurance.
- Prove that he knows what to do and has things under control.
- Prevent confusion and social fragmentation.
- Resist depression and sense of failure caused by the loss of the yacht.

Post a lookout

It is essential to post a lookout as soon as possible. They must:

- Look for any missing survivors in the water.
- Watch for other survival craft, SAR vessels, ships or aircraft.
- Scan the water for useful debris.

Open equipment pack

Carefully open the liferaft equipment; every item in your liferaft is valuable and irreplaceable. Check the grab bag and whatever else everyone managed to bring before you abandoned ship. If you have an extensive survival kit, look just far enough to find the search and rescue items and anything else you need immediately, consulting the list in your grab bag. A full inventory can wait.

Issue anti-seasickness medicine and seasickness bags

If there was no time to take anti-seasickness tablets whilst on the yacht, take some immediately. Keep taking these pills for the first 48 hours to avoid any risk of sickness and the resultant loss of body fluid. The pills often cause a dry mouth; unless water supplies are plentiful do not issue anything to drink. Anyone affected by seasickness should:

- Put their head down between their knees.
- Try to keep warm.
- Use disposable bags, reducing the smell of vomit that often causes others to be sick.

Dry liferaft floor and inflate, if appropriate

Inevitably, a liferaft will be wet and in rough conditions it is likely to continue getting wet. Bail out as much water as possible and sponge out the rest, reserving at least one sponge if possible. Keep this sponge separate to mop up any condensation as it forms, because this can supplement the water supplies.

In cold conditions, inflate the floor of the raft with the hand pump. If your raft does not have an insulated floor try to find something to sit on, such as the cockpit cushions.

Administer first aid, if appropriate

Check the physical condition of everyone aboard and give first aid where necessary, remembering the ABCs:

A is for Airway: is it clear?
B is for Breathing: is he?
C for Circulation, is the heart beating? Is there bleeding?

For more information, refer to the first aid notes in Chapter 8.

Manoeuvre towards other liferafts

If there are other liferafts it is important to link them together. Two or more liferafts are much easier for searchers to locate so connect rafts together with lines. Attach the lines to strong points, eg the painter attachment patch. Allow 15 m (50 ft) length or as necessary, to ensure rafts are on wave crests together.

Distribute survivors between the rafts and share out equipment.

Arrange watches and duties

The **Skipper** should:

- Establish who is available for watches, note any injuries and establish the expertise available on board.
- Arrange watches in pairs for about one hour, with an outside lookout and

an inside watch if numbers and weather conditions permit.
- Ensure that everyone knows how to keep a lookout and how and when to use all the signalling equipment.
- See that everyone has something to do and is involved when not resting, even if it is only to bail and keep the raft dry.
- Take charge of water and food.
- If possible record the circumstances leading up to abandoning the yacht.
- Keep a log of events thereafter with times, duties organised, rations issued, first aid given and condition of survivors.

The **lookout** should be:
- Suitably dressed and protected from the elements, with a hat to give shade or warmth and sunglasses or a swimming mask in rough conditions.
- Well secured to the craft by his harness or a rope.
- Responsible for keeping a lookout for other survivors, ships, aircraft and land.
- Watchful for all dangers.
- Collecting any useful debris.
- Alerting everyone to the possibility of rain to collect for drinking.
- Checking for abrasion of liferaft and any attached lines.

The **inside watch** should:
- Look after anyone with injuries.
- Be in charge of the safety and security of all the survival equipment.
- Ensure the signal equipment, particularly the flares, are ready to hand.
- Take responsibility for raft maintenance including bailing, ventilation and repairs.
- Organise the collection of rainwater.
- Supervise the liferaft management while the skipper rests.

Check liferaft for correct operation and any damage

Liferafts are constructed to withstand exposure for 30 days afloat in all sea conditions without deterioration, but they are vulnerable to accidental damage.
- Remove anything sharp or rough from clothing.
- Check frequently for damage from friction of the soles of shoes.
- Take great care when using anything sharp especially in rough seas.
- Keep all gear stowed properly.
- A well trimmed liferaft will reduce wear so spread out evenly around the raft. Sit on the floor with backs to tubes – never sit on the tubes. Use handholds provided as necessary.
- Check regularly for abrasion from anything attached outside – sea anchor, containers of water, other rafts etc.

- Plug and repair holes as soon as possible following instructions provided with the repair kit in the liferaft emergency pack. Plug large holes, securing them with a hose clamp or string. Use a liferaft repair clamp if available for a quick, permanent repair.
- If a tube has been holed, ventilate the liferaft interior to remove any leaked carbon dioxide.

Check functioning of the canopy light and conserve power during daylight

A light on the top of the raft is a valuable aid to location at night. Check that it is functioning and switch it off during daylight hours as it only has a life of between 12 and 24 hours. If your liferaft has no light or the fitted one has failed, hopefully you will be able to attach the strobe light packed in your grab bag to the top of the raft.

Adjust canopy openings to give protection from the weather or to ventilate the liferaft as appropriate

The sea anchor attachment aligns the entrances out of the wind and spray. In warm conditions change the position of the sea anchor line so the raft lies into the wind, and open all accesses to give maximum ventilation. Even in cold weather some ventilation will be necessary to provide everyone with plenty of oxygen.

Prepare and use detection equipment including radio equipment

Ensure all signalling equipment is secured at hand, ready for immediate use. The various methods of attracting attention are discussed here; for how to use them once help is close at hand, see Chapter 9.

EPIRB

If your EPIRB is not already on, switch it on now.
- Do not switch the beacon off until instructed by SAR authorities.
- Do not turn the unit off and on, to preserve the batteries; it will confuse the rescue authorities and will make the final homing very difficult.
- EPIRBs are designed to float outside the raft attached by a thin line. Ensure the knot is very secure, and check frequently for wear on line and raft. In rough weather consider bringing the unit inside the raft.
- If the beacon is kept inside the raft, ensure the liferaft does not have metal foil or metallic lining which could interfere with the signal. You should:
  - hold or attach the unit with the antenna vertical;
  - cover the strobe light to prevent driving the raft occupants crazy;
  - consider putting the unit outside at night, as the strobe is very effective at guiding rescuers.

SART

Turn the beacon on immediately, it will operate for 96 hours in stand-by mode and in excess of 8 hours in operational mode. This should be sufficient time for someone to reach you except in very remote areas. Attach it as high as possible using:

- its own pole
- the man overboard marker buoy from the yacht
- anything else available.
- Listen for the unit's alarm when it is interrogated by a nearby radar. This is a great morale booster and will alert you to the likelihood of rescuers arriving. It will also give you time to prepare other methods of signalling your whereabouts.

Radar reflector

If you are carrying a radar reflector this should be deployed, like a SART, as high as possible in such a position so as to best reflect the radar signal generated by rescue craft. However, SARTs and radar reflectors conflict with each other and both should not be deployed at the same time.

Portable VHF radio

Conserving your VHF batteries is the priority:

- Send a Mayday as soon as possible, especially if you had previously made contact with potential rescuers.
- Keep sending distress signals at regular intervals, even if you do not receive a reply.
- If the battery is getting low, reserve the VHF until help is close by.
- With a plentiful supply of batteries keep the unit on constantly and send frequent Maydays.

Pyrotechnics

Flares should not be used unless it is certain that help is nearby, and then only when a ship is as close to you as you think she is likely to get, or, in the case of an aircraft in daytime, when it is actually sighted. Take great care, flares are dangerous; they can easily hole a liferaft or give you a nasty burn, and have even killed people.

Signalling light

Like a flare, this is best used once help is close by, as it must be aimed in the direction of the rescuers to be effective. A strobe light attached to the liferaft will be useful for all round vision and has the benefit of not needing any supervision, but its range is more limited.

Signalling mirror

A signal mirror is inexhaustible and can be seen for miles; the record rescue from a mirror is just over 100 miles. During the daytime the lookout can catch the sunlight on the mirror and reflect it around the horizon, with practise 270º can be covered with one mirror. Do not try to use the mirror for Morse code, as the liferaft is unlikely to be stable enough.

Kite

If your grab bag includes a parafoil rescue kite, fly it during the daytime. Tie on the radar reflector if the wind is suitable as the higher you can suspend this the better. It may be possible to use the kite at night to lift up a strobe light.

Portable telephones

If you do have a mobile telephone of any kind, try to call the rescue services.

Gather up any useful floating objects

All useful debris should be collected; almost anything may have value later as an aid to survival. The most important items are those that can be used for signalling, such as EPIRBs or SARTs. Heavy articles with sharp edges should not be taken aboard as they could damage the raft.

Protect against heat, cold and wet conditions

Heat

It is essential in hot weather to keep as cool as possible to reduce perspiration and minimise dehydration. Use the cooling effect of the sea as follows:
- do not inflate the floor of the raft;
- regularly wet the liferaft canopy;
- wet clothes with seawater, but bear in mind damp clothes increase susceptibility to skin sores or salt-water boils;
- ensure clothes are dry by dusk; nights can be cool even in the tropics.
- Do not be tempted to swim, as sharks may be in the shade under the raft. You may be too weak to re-board the raft.
- Attach the sea anchor at the liferaft entrance to benefit from any breeze.
- Keep as still as possible.
- Stay in any shade; cover head, neck and exposed areas.
- Use sunscreen and sunglasses, especially the lookout.
- Remember reflection from the water can also cause sunburn.

Cold and wet

In cold climates it is vitally important to try to keep as warm and dry as possible.
- Remove wet clothing, wring out and put back on.
- Distribute spare dry clothes.

- Keep the raft as dry as possible.
- Adjust the openings for the minimum ventilation.
- Huddle together for mutual warmth but do not upset the trim of the raft.
- Sit on something to protect against the cold water; use a lifejacket to sit on in calm seas but wear the lifejacket in rough conditions.
- Use Thermal Protective Aids (TPAs) as they will reflect back 90 per cent of the body heat; feet will remain dry even in a partly water-filled liferaft.

Allocate TPAs to the coldest crew first; if two can fit in one bag, bundle a warmer person in with a cold individual.

Once warm, open up the top layer of clothing, so body warmth acts like a radiator to keep the whole raft cosy. Stretch limbs, wriggle toes and fingers,to maintain blood circulation and avoid cold injury.

In very cold conditions, rotate the lookout watch at frequent intervals.

Decide on food and water rations

At best, your liferaft emergency pack will have $1^1/_2$ litres (53 fl oz) of water per person; at worst, none at all.

The minimum daily amount of water considered necessary to survive in good shape is:
- 1 litre (35 fl oz) in the tropics.
- $^1/_2$ litre (18 fl oz) in temperate climates.
- 55 to 220 cc (2 to 5 oz) for a short period.

The emergency food rations, if available, should be divided:
- 100–125 gm (3–4 oz) per person per day.
- Distribute at the same time as the water ration.

Unless fresh water is plentiful and you know rescue is on the way, divide the agreed ration thus:

First day: No water or food, except for the sick, injured, near drowned, or very young.
Second day and thereafter: Agreed ration divided into three parts.
Last day minus one: Half the normal ration.

Regardless of how soon you expect to be rescued:

- Collect all rainwater.
- Start making water with a handheld watermaker immediately.
- Use made water and any from the yacht first. The water in a liferaft pack will keep indefinitely.
- Do not eat anything unless you can also have a drink.
- Do not drink urine; it can kill you.
- The general rule is **do not** drink seawater (see Chapter 6).

Issue food and water at set times each day to give everyone something to look forward to: sunrise, midday and sunset make good times. Cut foil water pouches with scissors as tearing risks losing precious water. For morale, rations must be seen to be issued fairly; a minimum daily water ration should be $1/2$ (18 fl oz) litre more for the injured. Water should be swilled round the mouth before being swallowed slowly.

Food rations should be distributed to last as long as possible. Do not eat anything caught unless 1 litre (35 fl oz) of water can be drunk per day.

Take measures to maintain morale

Morale and the will to survive are very important. Morale will probably be lowest about three hours after abandoning your yacht. Seasickness, anxiety, extreme cold and the absence of food or water will further lower morale. Always make sure that ration issues are fair and on time.

Keep peoples' minds focused on eventual rescue and attracting attention; never talk of defeat or death in the liferaft. Use anything and everything to keep everyone cheerful including competitions, card games, songs and jokes. Listen to commercial broadcasts if you have a radio.

People with a strong will to survive can overcome seemingly impossible difficulties.

Make sanitary arrangements to keep the liferaft habitable

To avoid problems everyone should:
- Attempt to urinate within two hours of boarding the raft.
- Attempt a bowel movement within the first 24 hours.
- In calm seas, rig a safety line to aid defaecation and urination over the side.
- In rough seas, use a bailer, bucket or other receptacle.
- Use the special sick bags from the liferaft pack or any plastic bag.
- Clean up all waste and throw it over the side immediately.
- If sharks are around, however, be careful about disposing of anything over the side.

Maintain the liferaft including topping up buoyancy tubes and canopy supports

It is important to your survival that the liferaft is kept in good condition. A properly inflated liferaft is less likely to wear. Use plugs in top-up valves when not in use.

In hot weather remove plugs regularly to allow excess pressure to escape and ensure adequate ventilation to avoid a build-up of carbon dioxide.

At night and on cooler days top up soft buoyancy tubes and canopy supports.

Make proper use of available survival equipment

Everyone must understand:

- How to use all equipment especially signalling devices.
- The importance of all the search and rescue equipment for ultimate rescue.
- The potential to damage the raft with equipment, such as flares.
- The necessity of preserving every item in perfect condition and inside the liferaft, by returning it to the stowage position or fastening it to himself, herself or the liferaft by means of a lanyard.

Prepare actions for arrival of rescue units, being taken in tow, rescue by helicopter and landing and beaching

Everyone aboard the liferaft, especially the lookout, must be ready for the possible arrival of SAR units or the sighting of land. Rescue can arrive by air as well as by sea. The ocean is large and a liferaft very small and hard to see, especially in rough weather. Proper use of any or all of the signalling equipment will help attract attention. See Chapter 9 for more information.

REMEMBER: NO ONE IS A SURVIVOR UNTIL THEY HAVE BEEN RESCUED

6

LONG-TERM SURVIVAL IN A LIFERAFT

With good communication equipment on board your yacht and an EPIRB or two in your liferaft, this chapter is probably superfluous. Unfortunately, as they say 'the best laid plans of mice and men....' and there are still wild and lonely places in the world where few others sail. The SAR authorities may be on their way; a fixed wing aircraft may sight you, but rescue by helicopter or boat may be delayed.

As the hours pass it is essential to keep up morale and to maintain a vigilant lookout at all times. Good liferaft management should continue right up to the moment you leave the liferaft. As the days pass without rescue, water and food will become increasingly important and it may be necessary to move the liferaft.

WATER

Water is essential for long-term survival. If rescue does not arrive quickly, what water you have aboard quickly becomes depleted, so where and how much more can be acquired becomes the priority. A healthy person can live without water for 7–10 days and without food for 20–30 days in temperate conditions. The body naturally loses water: 50 per cent as urine; 25 per cent as water vapour during respiration; 25 per cent as sweat. You also lose water as a result of seasickness and digestion. By reducing the amount of water the body loses, you reduce the amount you need.

Reduced urine

By not drinking water for the first 24 hours in the liferaft, the body's automatic response to reduced water intake will initiate reduced urine production.

Reduced respiration and sweat

Practise all the points included in Chapter 5 under Protection against heat. The less you move, particularly in the tropics, the less water you will sweat out or expel in respiration.

If your liferaft has no canopy, create shade using whatever you have available such as oars, blankets and clothes.

Pay special attention to protection for the lookout.

Reduced seasickness

Vomiting leads to both dehydration and exhaustion and must be avoided at all costs. Use all the measures discussed in Chapter 5 under Issue Anti-seasickness Medicine. If possible take anti-seasickness pills during the first storm, especially if sea conditions were calm earlier. Do not eat if you feel sick.

Drinking urine

Urine contains poisonous waste products which the body has already discarded. It is of no use and urine must not be drunk. At best, your body will have to get rid of the waste again and this will take more water. Do not believe anyone who suggests someone else's urine is acceptable: they are lying, and it is just as bad for you as for them.

Drinking seawater

Drinking seawater is considered dangerous and will result in kidney failure. The salt in seawater must be dissolved using water from the body so that the kidneys can pass the salt into the urine. This sets up a vicious circle; the more salt water is drunk the more fresh water is taken from the body cells to dissolve the salt. But it has been proved that it is possible to survive on seawater, to stay alive if not healthy.

In 1952 a Frenchman, Dr Alain Bombard, concluded that survival at sea without fresh water would be possible by pressing liquid from fish and edible marine organic matter. To prove this he sailed from Casablanca to Barbados in a rubber dinghy with no food or water. He drank seawater for 14 days, in consecutive periods of 3 to 6 days maximum. The French Navy followed this with more research and concluded that seawater could be drunk under certain conditions:

- Seawater must be drunk immediately while the body is hydrated and thirst has not set in.
- Drink a maximum of 900 cc (32 fl oz) per day.
- Fresh water must be drunk after about 3 days to flush the excess salt from the body.
- Do not exceed 5 days of drinking seawater alone.
- Do not drink seawater if already dehydrated.

Supplementing the water ration

The importance of supplementing water rations cannot be overstressed. Rationing is uncomfortable; saliva will disappear, lips will crack and you will feel weak. If delirium starts this is a sign that more water is urgently needed to sustain life. A watermaker (a manually operated reverse osmosis water pump) is, after the EPIRB, the most valuable item aboard your liferaft. Your next most likely source of fresh water comes from rain, followed by ice and condensation.

Collecting rainwater

Depending on location, rain can occur daily, occasionally or rarely. Unless rain is a daily occurrence, it is very important to be ready to take advantage of it. Lookouts must alert everyone to impending rain.

Leave rain-catching equipment ready before nightfall as sleepiness and darkness may make it harder to take advantage of a short rain shower. At the first sign of rain, remove salt crystallised over catchment areas by washing with seawater.

Use any large piece of fabric to catch rain such as sails, large plastic bags, heavy weather gear etc. Cans and bottles make good containers but not good collectors. Some liferaft canopies have drainage tubes leading inside through which rainwater can be directed into containers.

Keep catching equipment out of the sea to prevent contamination. However, in rough seas it may be impossible to collect uncontaminated fresh water.

Use every available container for storage – buckets, bailer, plastic bag etc. Keep the first water collected separately as it will probably contain a little salt. Use it to clean wounds or sores and wash off your skin. If rainfall persists and every container is full, use the excess for personal hygiene.

Drink rainwater slowly to prevent vomiting if you are on strict rationing.

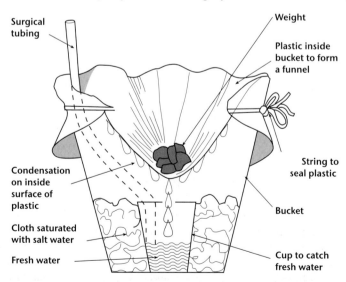

A solar still can be made from a bucket, a cup and a plastic bag.

Collecting ice

In the polar regions ice of various kinds is available:

- Old ice, a year or more old, will be free or nearly free of salt. Old ice is bluish, has rounded corners and splinters easily; new ice is grey, milky and hard.
- Water from icebergs is fresh, but they are dangerous to approach and should only be viewed as a source of fresh water in an emergency.
- If it is very cold, freeze seawater in containers. Salt will freeze last and will concentrate in the middle. Then break ice from the sides only to get low saline water.
- Collect any ice off the surface of various pieces of equipment; it is fresh water, frozen condensation.

Other water sources

In dry places with little rain, night time brings copious condensation. Water may condense under the liferaft canopy or exposure cover. Keep some sponges or cloths separately and use only to collect this water.

Some parts of fish contain fresh water. Cut them in half and drink the spinal fluid. You can also suck the liquid from the eyes of large fish.

Do not drink any other body liquids; they are rich in proteins and fat and will use more water to digest than you can gain from the fluid.

Solar stills and desalting tablets are included in some liferafts. Set up a solar still as soon as possible. They are slow to produce water and will only work on flat calm seas.

Using foul water

Foul water is usually safe to drink but it may be so unpalatable that it causes retching. Up to $1/2$ l (18 fl oz) can be absorbed rectally using an enema. In severe dehydration, an enema is often the best way of rehydrating the body. Do not use salt water for this purpose; it is as dangerous rectally as orally.

FOOD

The digestion of food requires a lot of water; do not eat if you cannot drink. Over a short period you can survive without food. Over a long period you need to eat for energy and health. Protein requires more water to digest than carbohydrates. Since everything you are likely to catch contains protein, do eat anything caught without at least 1 litre (35 fl oz) of water per day. If water supplies are low, eat survival craft rations which are specially designed to require little water. Also eat carbohydrates such as sugars and starches. Do not eat proteins or anything dried.

Very little waste residue results from eating emergency rations, so do not worry if you become constipated; this will also prevent the loss of valuable body water.

Supplementing the food ration

If fresh water is plentiful, eat any food brought from the yacht, or caught, before using liferaft emergency rations. The sources of additional food at sea are limited to fish, birds, seaweed, turtles, shellfish and possibly plankton. With adequate water, the sea can provide enough food to sustain life for a long time. Eating fish alone may cause vitamin deficiencies, so if you have multivitamin tablets in your grab bag take them regularly. With ingenuity, most of what is around you in a liferaft can be used to catch, attract or find food.

Catching fish

Fish are plentiful in most oceans and can be caught relatively easily; flying fish may even throw themselves at you. If you cannot or do not want to eat the fish you catch for some reason, such as other available food or lack of water, continue to fish as this can act as a morale booster and it never hurts to practise a skill that may, in time, be needed to sustain life.

Improvisation can turn a number of items into fishing equipment, for example:
- Line from unravelled threads or rope.
- Hooks from metal, plastic etc.
- Lures from any shiny metal, feathers, the intestines of an earlier catch etc.
- A spear from a knife tied very securely to an oar.
- A gaff from your largest hook attached to an oar.

It is very easy to damage an inflatable liferaft so be careful with anything sharp such as hooks and spears. Fish can jump and harm the liferaft, as well as disappearing over the side. Do not try to land anything too large. Better to go hungry than end up swimming because the raft has sunk.

Fishing equipment is easy to lose so tie everything very carefully. If possible, include a line back to the raft or held by another person. Do not throw a spear that has your only knife attached to it.

Line fishing
Use small fish as a lure to catch bigger relatives and keep bait moving in the water so it looks alive.

Spear fishing
Throw the spear straight down into the water not at an angle, to avoid refraction errors. Once spiked, land fish quickly to prevent it slipping back off the blade. Tie the eye of the hook to the raft in case the hook comes off the shaft.

Gaffing

Put the gaff in the water, hook upwards, and wait for a victim to swim by. Aim for the stomach and get the fish straight on board as fast as possible.

Speargun fishing

A proper speargun is by far the easiest method of catching fish; you use it in the same way as a spear. Be very careful as you bring it back aboard the raft so as not to tear it. Spearguns can be used to land or kill large fish caught by line.

Attracting fish

By day fish may be lurking under the raft, attracted by the shade. By night use an electric light or try reflecting the light of a full moon using a signalling mirror.

Flying fish are found in schools and a light will attract them. Hold a light coloured sheet vertically, even during the day; as they fly over the fish will hit it and fall stunned into the raft, in theory at least.

Using your catch

Most fish caught in the open sea are likely to be edible. Healthy fish can safely be eaten raw; it is a delicacy in many countries and you can eat everything except the intestines.

Poisonous fish are usually found in coastal areas, particularly reefs. The dangerous types have spines, spikes, bristles or puff themselves up. Some can be eaten if the internal organs are discarded but, like eating toadstools and mushrooms, do not attempt it unless you are sure. If you must eat poisonous fish to survive, only eat flesh that has not been in contact with organs and do not touch the spines with bare hands. Eat a small amount, wait a few hours for any adverse reactions, then eat more.

Fish should be gutted and bled as soon as possible after catching. In hot weather eat within half a day or dry, especially dark meat. Never eat fish with pale, shiny gills, sunken eyes, flabby skin or flesh, or an unpleasant odour. Good fish are the opposite and have a saltwater or clean fishy odour.

To dry fish or anything else caught, hang up fillets in the sun, or cut into thin slices and lay out in the sun. High humidity can make it hard to dry food successfully.

When eating dried fish or meat, you should only consume it with a plentiful supply of water. Check very carefully to make sure it is not rotten, and if green or slime develops, scrape off and redry. If the flesh is disintegrating throw it away. Leftover fish or anything doubtful can be used as bait.

Birds

All sea birds are edible although the taste may not be attractive and they can take a lot of chewing. They can be caught most successfully by hand, hook, spear or snare. If a bird lands on your raft for a rest, grab it quickly and wring its neck.

The easiest way to catch a bird is with a hook and line: attach fish or meat to the hook and float it on the water; when the hook is taken pull in the line.

To spear a bird place a bit of cloth or bright metal on the water near the raft. When the bird lands, throw the spear (attached to a line).

To snare a bird make a large lasso from rope that will float. Spread out the loop on water, holding the end of the rope. Place a bit of cloth or bright metal in the centre of the noose, then when the bird lands tighten the noose.

Using your catch
- Skin a bird and eat everything except the intestines.
- Break the bones to extract the marrow.
- Entrails, feet and feathers can be used as bait.
- Fat under the bird's skin can lubricate your skin.
- In cold weather feathers can be used as insulation and fat is a valuable food.

Turtles

Sea turtle meat is very nutritious and they offer a major source of food if they can be caught. It may be environmentally unfriendly to eat them, but when you are hungry enough you will overcome your feelings. The best way to catch and kill a turtle is:
- Grab or gaff it by the hind flippers.
- Turn it onto its back, pull it on board and cut its throat.
- Take great care, the beak or claws on the flippers can damage rafts.

Using your catch
The blood should be drunk before it coagulates; it is a valuable source of nourishment and tastes good. Cut the top shell from the bottom to get to meat found mostly around the legs. Eat the meat at once; it may go bad quickly especially in humid weather, but leftover meat can be dried. Bones should be broken to extract the marrow. Eggs inside a female turtle are excellent food, a delicacy in many tropical islands.

Seaweed

Most seaweeds are edible although salty. They are a good source of protein, vitamins, minerals and fibre. You must have water to rinse and drink with seaweed. If you do not have enough, collect the seaweed and dry it, to await sufficient water. Even if the seaweed is too tough to eat raw, inspect every bit that passes the raft carefully for small fish or crabs that can be eaten.

Plankton

Plankton is very nutritious and will be found in any area where whales live. It is easiest to get at night when it is near the surface. It looks like grey scum and is best mixed with something else, but it will provide valuable protection from scurvy.

A towed net is needed to collect plankton and ideally a speed of about 2 knots. A specially made net is best but you can improvise with any material, and a spare sea anchor makes a perfect plankton net.

Barnacles

Without any antifouling your liferaft will soon grow barnacles, and in a few weeks they will be big enough to eat. These will also grow on any lines trailing in the water and will be easier to get at than those under the raft. Eat barnacles whole; the shell also provides nutrition.

PROTECTION

If the time aboard the liferaft is measured in days rather than hours, it becomes even more important to take care of your rather delicate vessel. Unlike a yacht, rafts are manufactured for just days of use rather than years. Wear is the biggest problem, and any line or object that touches an inflatable raft has the potential to eventually wear a hole. It is important to try to prevent this by padding and changing their position.

Outside the raft, problems may come from sea creatures underneath. As the time in the water increases, rafts without antifouling are susceptible to weed and barnacles and these are attractive to turtles, fish and sharks. Whilst anything touching the raft is frightening, this may have a positive side, such as an opportunity to catch dinner.

Sharks

Sharks are creatures that invoke fear in most sailors despite the softer picture projected by recent nature films. There are sharks in every ocean, and while many live and feed in the depths, others hunt near the surface. When you are in the liferaft and see sharks:

- Do not throw anything overboard by day; wait until it is dark.
- Do not fish and if you have hooked a fish, discard it.
- Do not let arms, legs or equipment hang in the water.
- Make sure everyone keeps quiet and still.
- Do not attempt to kill shark for food except as a last resort; they are very difficult to land without damaging oneself or the liferaft. Do not bring a shark aboard the raft until it is dead. Cut off the head and skin immediately. Do not eat the liver as it is poisonous.

If a shark attack is imminent, hit it with anything except your hands. Be careful not to break or lose the article you use.

Heavy weather

Weather watching must not be limited to seeking rain clouds to supplement drinking water. It is also important for the lookout to be alert to worsening conditions that could be a serious danger and it is important that everyone is ready for the rough time ahead and that:

- Lifejackets are worn.
- Anti-seasickness tablets are taken.
- Sea anchors are deployed, and a second anchor prepared for use.
- All equipment is stowed or tied on with lanyards.
- Entrances are closed to prevent water entering.
- Crew are evenly distributed around the liferaft with backs against the tubes and feet into the centre.
- If the liferaft is not full, crew should sit to windward to aid stability.

In very rough conditions a second sea anchor can be streamed. If this is necessary, ensure the drogues' lines are of different length to prevent fouling.

LOCATION

In the past the decision to stay at the scene of the sinking or to try to move away was more debatable. Now, with modern communications, particularly satellite equipment, making it likely that help is on its way, it rarely makes sense to move, even if it were possible to 'sail' a liferaft. Strong currents may move the raft rapidly away from the wreck, and if the wind is favourable it may be possible and sensible to sail back to the position of the disaster. It is important to remember that if a Mayday was sent from the yacht and not answered, that does not mean it has not been heard and the centre of the search will always be the yacht's last position.

Once in the liferaft the best method of communicating distress is a 406 MHz or Inmarsat E EPIRB. If the unit ceases to function before rescue is achieved, SAR authorities will use its last known position as the focus of the search area. If you have no EPIRB or it is not working and you did not manage to make a distress call, an attempt to move away from the scene might be valid if:

- The yacht has sunk and all useful items have floated to the surface.
- No one ashore will miss you and you did not leave a Voyage Details Plan.
- If five days have passed without help arriving.
- There is land, shipping or fishing boats nearby.
- The wind and/or current is in the right direction.
- There is very little water and no rain expected.
- It is possible to 'sail' the raft.

Any decision to move away must be discussed and good reasons given to the crew to ensure their support, which is vital to the success of the venture.

Moving a liferaft

Sailing a liferaft is difficult because they are not designed to do this. One manufacturer does make a sailing liferaft, but it is a dinghy first and a liferaft second. Current and wind will affect the raft's progress – a portable GPS will be very helpful in monitoring this movement. With the sea anchor rigged:

• The current is the main influence on the movement of a liferaft.
• The lower the raft is in the water the greater the effect.
• Ordinary liferafts do not have keels and cannot be sailed into the wind. Therefore direction of travel will be downwind, or slightly off that, otherwise there is no point in attempting to rig a sail.

If you do decide to sail, ensure the liferaft is fully inflated; take in the sea anchor, use an oar as a rudder and rig a sail and/or experiment with the liferaft openings.

If you decide to head for land, unless it is in sight choose a land target that is large. A small island may be near but is all too easy to miss. When land is in sight use any onshore wind in the mornings and possibly the afternoons. Use the sea anchor at night to stop an offshore breeze pushing you away.

If you need water, the longer wind travels over water, the more vapour it will pick up. Downwind is usually the direction towards rain in the middle of the ocean.

PSYCHOLOGICAL DISINTEGRATION

As time passes in a liferaft it is all too easy for psychological problems to increase just as easily as the physical problems of surviving. Denial can lead to apathy, apathy to depressed reaction, depressed reaction to despair and despair to psychological disintegration. Once that final stage is reached death is not far away.

The initial symptoms include irritability, sleep disturbance and mild startle reaction. Later comes social withdrawal, loss of interest, apprehension, general mental and physical retardation, confusion and finally death. Death, when it comes, can be a passive sinking or it can suddenly be considered a serious option, with suicide an easier alternative to the struggle to live. This breakdown can happen to an individual but it can also affect a group. It can develop progressively or a particular event can act as a sudden trigger.

One common event that can severely upset survivors in a liferaft is to watch a potential rescue craft fail to sight the raft and then turn away. At such times a strong leader may be all that keeps a group functioning and fighting on. A fierce determination to live, the willingness to improvise and regular activity, both mental and physical, can overcome most things. Water and food may be scarce but they can be found in most areas, and with rationing life can go on. The strengths of each member of the group add to that of the others and increase the chance for everyone to reach the ultimate goal of rescue and survival.

7

INITIAL FIRST AID AND EMERGENCY TREATMENT

A first aid kit is supplied with some liferaft packs. Hopefully you will also have brought the medical box from your yacht. This section provides basic information on emergency treatment of injuries and other immediate medical problems that may need to be dealt with aboard a liferaft.

GENERAL ASSESSMENT

With any patient, it is important to make a rapid examination to assess responsiveness and the extent of the injury:
- If the patient is unconscious go straight to the Unconscious section
- If there is serious bleeding go to the Bleeding section.
- Handle the patient as little and as gently as possible so as to prevent further injuries and further shock.
- Place the patient in the most comfortable position possible and loosen tight clothing so that they can breathe easily.
- Do not remove more clothing than is necessary and be as gentle as possible.
- With an injured limb, get the sound limb out of the clothing first then peel the clothes off the injured limb, which should be supported by another person during the process.

Shock can be a great danger to life, especially in the case of liferaft survivors, and one of the main objects of first aid is to prevent this.

Once it has been established that there is no immediate threat to life there will be time to decide what treatment is possible in the liferaft. It is very important to be reassuring and compassionate even though there may be little that can be actively done to provide a cure.

UNCONSCIOUSNESS

The immediate threat to life may be:
- Breathing obstructed by the tongue falling back and blocking the throat.
- Stopped heart.

It is important to remember the ABCs:
A is for Airway
B is for Breathing
C is for Circulation

A is for Airway

This means establishing an open airway, by tilting the forehead back so that the casualty can breathe easily.
1 Lay casualty flat on his back.
2 Place your hand on the casualty's forehead.
3 Place the fingers of your other hand under the chin.
4 Tilt the head and lift the jaw.
5 Open the mouth and remove any obvious obstructions such as blood, vomit or secretions with your fingers or a clean piece of cloth.
6 Only remove any dentures if they are broken or displaced.

These actions may relieve the obstruction to breathing. The casualty may gasp and start to breathe naturally. If so, go on to the Recovery Position section.

B is for Breathing

Check for breathing – Look/Listen/Feel for 3 to 5 seconds:
- Look for movements of the chest and abdomen.
- Feel for the patient's breathing on your cheek.
- Listen for breathing with your ear over the mouth and nose.
- Note the colour of face and lips – normal or blue/grey tinge?

Not breathing
Begin **artificial respiration** at once – seconds count. **Never give rescue breathing to a person who is breathing normally.**
1 Check the airway remains open using head tilt and chin lift.
2 Move to one side of the patient.
3 Pinch the casualty's nose with your finger and thumb. After taking a full breath, seal you lips about the patient's mouth and blow into his mouth for about 2 seconds until you see the chest rise.
4 If a barrier device is available use it. In water use mouth to nose.

81

5 Give two effective inflations quickly, then note if the colour of the face and lips is improving.

If there is improvement, continue the artificial respiration, at a rate of about 12 inflations each minute (count to five, slowly, between inflations). When the patient commences breathing go on to Recovery Position section.
   If there is no improvement:
• Listen for heart sounds.
• Feel the pulse in the neck.
• Check for any coughing or movement of the chest.

If no heartbeat is found, the heart has stopped; begin CPR at once. You have at best, 4 to 6 minutes to restore circulation.

C is for circulation and CPR (cardio-pulmonary resuscitation)

The casualty must be on a hard surface for CPR to be effective, which may be difficult in a liferaft.
1 Kneel, facing the casualty's chest.
2 With your fingers locate the lower edge of the ribcage on the side closest to you.
3 Slide your fingers up the ribcage to the notch at the end of the breastbone.
4 Place your middle finger on the notch, and your index finger next to it.
5 Place the heel of your other hand on the breastbone next to your index finger.
6 Place the heel of the hand used to locate the notch on top of the heel of your other hand, interlocking the fingers if desired.
7 Position shoulders over your hands, with elbows locked and arms straight.
8 Press firmly to produce a downward movement of about 4 cm ($1^1/_2$ to 2 in). Repeat rapidly at the rate of 100 times a minute.
9 Artificial respiration must be continued when giving heart compression since breathing stops when the heart stops.
   • When administering CPR give 15 compressing thrusts then 2 deep breaths.

Check for response: if the heart starts to beat, the colour of the face and lips will improve and the eye pupils will get smaller. Listen again for heart sounds and feel for a neck pulse after 1 minute and then at 3-minute intervals. If they are heard, stop heart compression but continue with artificial respiration until natural breathing is restored.
   When you are satisfied that the heart is beating and the patient is breathing naturally, carry on to the Recovery Position section.

Even in a fully equipped hospital with a team of trained doctors, CPR is not always successful. Attempting CPR can do no further harm; the patient is dead if you do not make an attempt. Try to continue the process for at least one hour. **Never** consider anyone to be dead until you and everyone else in the liferaft agrees that:

- Breathing has stopped and cannot be restarted.
- No pulse is felt and no sounds are heard when your ear is put to the chest.
- The eyes are glazed and pupils are dilated.
- There is a progressive cooling of the body.

Recovery position

Place the casualty in the unconscious or recovery position to keep the airway clear.

- Turn patient onto one side.
- To keep body in a stable position, bend and pull up leg and the arm on the side to which the head is facing.
- Pull up chin to give clear airway. Keep mouth downwards to avoid choking. Stretch other arm out along the other side of the body.
- In the liferaft it may be necessary to wedge the patient in this position using lifejackets and possibly lash them in place.
- Any carbon dioxide build up in the liferaft will be very dangerous for an unconscious casualty. Watch carefully for any gas leaking from the buoyancy tubes and keep the raft well ventilated.
- Loosen clothing and remove any false teeth or spectacles.
- Do not give fluids or anything else to eat or drink.
- Treat for shock when the casualty regains consciousness.

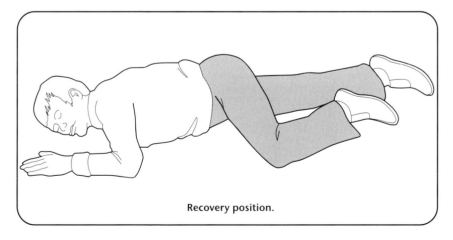

Recovery position.

NEAR DROWNING

Immediately treat any unconscious victims as described in the Unconsciousness section. Immersion victims may vomit during or immediately after resuscitation, due to the amount of water they have swallowed and/or the inadvertent distension of the stomach, particularly if the neck was not well extended.

- Check the casualty's airway frequently to ensure that it remains clear.
- Do not try to drain water from the lungs of near-drowned victims.
- Give extra water rations as soon as they can drink to avoid dehydration.
- Casualty may also need to be treated for hypothermia.

Victims recovered from cold water near to drowning may show all the symptoms of death:

- Blue skin.
- No detectable breathing.
- No apparent pulse or heartbeat.
- Pupils wide open.

They may not be dead; the body may have gone into the mammalian diving reflex. For this to happen the water temperature must be less than 21°C (70°F), the face must have been immersed and the victim will probably be young.

Many children have been successfully resuscitated from freezing water after 30 minutes as the blood is diverted from the arms and legs to circulate between the heart, brain and lungs.

- Do not give up until the body has warmed up but still shows no sign of life.
- Give artificial respiration if hypothermia is suspected.
- Be sure all pulse is absent before you start CPR (see the Hypothermia setion).

BLEEDING

Severe bleeding must be stopped as soon as possible. Action to be taken:

- Lay the casualty down.
- Clear away any clothing to expose the wound.
- Do not use a tourniquet.
- Press where the blood comes from, using a clean handkerchief, dressing or cloth for 5 to 15 minutes.
- Do not remove anything embedded in the wound; instead apply pressure beside the fragment.
- Press down hard with your hand or fist on the wound if nothing else is available. If possible wear disposable gloves.
- If direct pressure is impossible apply indirect pressure at a pressure point between the wound and the heart for a maximum of 15 minutes.

- Raise the bleeding part of the body to a near-vertical position if possible as this will help to stop the bleeding. Do not raise the limb if it is fractured.
- Bandage firmly around the wound to maintain the pressure, if necessary adding more padding if bleeding continues.
- Keep the injured part as still as possible and the casualty at rest because movement will disturb and destroy blood clots.

This treatment applies equally to bleeding from an amputation site, when pressure should be applied over and around the end of the stump.

Do not attempt to remove any foreign objects in a wound unless they are superficial and can easily be removed.

Internal bleeding

If internal bleeding is suspected lay the patient down with the feet raised, loosen clothing and treat them as for shock.

Chest wounds

A superficial chest wound should be treated as for any wound elsewhere. A penetrating wound, which makes a sucking sound, must be sealed immediately otherwise the lungs will not be able to inflate, as the vacuum inside the chest will be destroyed. Action to be taken:

- Temporarily plug the wound with the casualty's own bloodstained clothing.
- Cover the wound with a wet dressing or use petroleum jelly on gauze.
- Seal on three sides only so the dressing acts as a one-way valve: as the patient breathes in, the dressing sucks down on the wound, and as he breathes out the air can escape through the flap valve.

The usual rules about stopping bleeding by pressing where the blood comes from also apply. **Note: do not give morphine** to a patient with this type of wound, even if he is suffering from a lot of pain, because morphine will increase breathing difficulties.

Abdominal wounds

A superficial abdominal wound will require the same treatment as for any wound. For more serious wounds, take the following action:

- If the abdominal contents *do not protrude*, cover the wound with a large standard dressing and place the casualty in the half-sitting-up position, or flat if the wound runs more or less vertically.
- If the abdominal contents *do protrude* through the wound **do not attempt to put them back.** Cover with a loosely applied large standard dressing or dressings.

- Shock should be treated as below except:
  - Prop up if necessary.
  - **Do not** give anything by mouth.
  - If the patient is thirsty, moisten lips, but nothing more.

SHOCK

Shock is the result of, amongst other things, severe bleeding, injuries, burns, infections, heat exhaustion or lack of oxygen. The pulse becomes rapid and feeble; the skin is cold, clammy and paler than normal, often greyish. Dizziness, fainting, vomiting and unconsciousness can occur. The state of collapse is due to a reduction in the volume of blood circulating in the body caused by loss of blood, serum or fluids. Treat shock as follows:

- Stop the bleeding.
- Loosen clothes.
- Relieve pain.
- **Do not** give morphine when patient has breathing difficulties or severe head injuries.
- Cover with extra clothing but do not overwarm, especially if a lot of blood has been lost.
- Unless there are breathing difficulties, raise the legs of conscious patients.
- Reassure and encourage the patient.
- Be prepared to give artificial respiration and CPR.
- Place an unconscious victim in recovery position.

HYPOTHERMIA

Hypothermia is the term given to the condition when the deep body temperature is lowered below 35°C (95°F) and body functions become impaired. The rate of heat loss in water is many times greater than in air and will vary depending on the difference in temperature between the body and the water. Any time spent in the water is likely to produce some degree of hypothermia. Heat loss will occur in any water below 35.5°C (96°F). In tropical water death from hypothermia will take a considerable period, in colder waters it can occur in less than one hour.

Mild to moderate condition – 36 to 34°C (97–93°F)

The patient will suffer from:

- Shivering, cold hands and feet.
- Numbness in limbs, loss of dexterity, clumsiness.
- Irrational behaviour.
- Confusion, slurred speech.

Severe condition – 33 to 29°C (92–84°F)

The symptoms change to:
- Shivering decreases or stops.
- Further loss of reasoning and recall, confusion and abnormal behaviour.
- Muscle rigidity develops.
- Skin becomes pale and pupils dilate.
- Pulse rate and breathing decrease.
- Victim semiconscious to unconscious.

Critical condition – 28°C (82°F) and below

The patient's condition deteriorates:
- Breathing erratic and very shallow or may not be apparent.
- Victim is unconscious and may appear dead.
- Pulse slow and weak or no pulse may be found.
- Skin is cold, may be bluish-grey in colour.
- The body is very rigid.

In a liferaft you should, if possible, actively treat hypothermia as follows:
- Gently strip off all wet clothing and replace with dry, or wring out water and put back on.
- Use spare clothing, blankets or TPAs for seriously affected victims.
- Huddle together under any covering to conserve heat and re-warm.
- Place seriously affected victims in close proximity to warmer survivors.
- Place a warm person in a TPA together with a hypothermic survivor.
- Use chemical heat packs in the armpits, groin and either side of the neck before wrapping the victim up.
- Encourage the patient to urinate as body heat is wasted keeping urine warm.

But:
- **Never** rub or try to warm a hypothermic victim's limbs. This can send cold stagnant blood from the periphery to the core further decreasing core temperature. It can lead to death.
- **Do not** give any alcohol or allow the patient to exert himself.

For severe hypothermic victims:
- Check breathing and heart rate very carefully.
- Be sure all pulse is absent before you start CPR. Premature cardiac massage may actually precipitate cardiac arrest.
- Start artificial respiration if breathing appears to be absent in order to increase available oxygen. Warm air blown into the lungs will also assist internal re-warming.

- Begin active re-warming, but do not remove clothes and avoid excessive handling of the casualty.

Do not give up resuscitation too soon.

BURNS

All burns are serious but if the burned area exceeds 10 per cent of the body surface they are dangerous. Those exceeding 33 per cent of the body surface are often fatal. All burns create raw tissue susceptible to infection. The larger the area of body burned, the greater the shock and more seriously ill the patient.

Superficial (first degree) burns

These affect only the outer skin layers and cause reddening.
- Clean if necessary with fresh water.
- Leave open or cover with a clean dry dressing.

Moderate (second degree) burns

These cause reddening, blistering, swelling and weeping of fluids.
- Remove any constricting jewellery and clothing.
- Do not attempt to pull off any that are stuck.
- Wash the area with soap and fresh water, using a lint-free cloth.
- Do not touch with your hands.
- Do not burst any blisters.
- Cover with a paraffin gauze dressing then more gauze, cotton wool and a bandage.
- Loosen the dressing if swelling occurs.
- Do not disturb dressing for a week, unless it becomes very smelly, dirty or the patient's temperature is raised.
- Give the patient as much water as possible to replace lost body fluids.
- Treat for shock and administer pain medication.

Deep (third degree) burns

Deep burns will have destroyed all skin and may have penetrated to underlying fat, muscle and bone. There is little you can do for this condition, or any extensive burns, in a liferaft. Cover the area with clingfilm if available and treat as for moderate burns.

FRACTURES

Unless expert medical attention is available, little can be done for the patient in a liferaft except to immobilise the fracture with bandages, slings and splints.

- If nothing is available to make a splint use the patient's own body, eg strap a broken leg to whole one, use elephant (duct) tape with cloth or paper to stop it sticking to the skin. Do not strap so tightly that circulation is affected.
- Make the patient as comfortable as possible.
- Provide pain relief and treat them for shock.
- Prevent movement caused by rolling liferaft by placing patient between two fit survivors.

FUEL OIL CONTAMINATION

Survivors who have spent time in water that has been contaminated by fuel oil are likely to be affected by:

Swallowing oil

- Usually causes vomiting; the effect will wear off in a few days.
- Give milk or additional water to replace body fluid lost if vomiting.

Clogging of skin pores

- Oil on the skin should be cleaned off as far as possible.
- If totally smothered in oil skin cannot perspire or breathe; this can kill.

Pollution of lungs

- Little can be done in the raft.
- It can be dangerous and lead to pneumonia.
- Rest, warmth and fresh air are about the only treatment.

Inflammation of the eyes

- Wash out with seawater.
- Protect from bright sunlight until any inflammation has gone.

Treat any wounds as if the oil was not present.

PRESCRIPTION DRUGS

Be very cautious about taking any drugs whilst in the liferaft if water and food are in short supply. The way many drugs affect the body will be altered by dehydration. Be cautious about continuing to take regular medicines or courses of treatment started whilst aboard the yacht, unless not to do so would be life threatening.

8

AILMENTS

Living in a liferaft with little room and no real exercise is hard, even in perfect conditions where food and drink are plentiful, seas are calm and the weather is mild. In most cases perfect conditions will not prevail and people will suffer, especially if rescue is long delayed.

SEASICKNESS

While a feeling of nausea is almost inevitable in a liferaft either at first or during the first storm, actual seasickness must be avoided if at all possible. Some people are always more susceptible than others, but most eventually get used to the movements of a vessel after a few days and suffer less. Seasickness can cause:
- Extreme fluid loss and exhaustion.
- Depression and the loss of the will to live.
- Others to become nauseated.
- Sharks to be attracted to the liferaft.
- Unclean conditions.

Various ideas for reducing seasickness have been discussed in Chapters 3 and 5, though for some people the only real cure is to 'sit under a tree' – get off the liferaft.

Treatment for seasickness
- Wash the patient and the liferaft to remove the sight and smell of the vomit.
- Do not give the patient any food until the nausea has gone.
- Give flat cola type drinks to help settle the stomach and rehydration.
- Lay patient down for rest, covered with warm coats or blankets.
- Give patient anti-seasickness pills rectally if possible.
- Use prescription anti-emetic.

COLD INJURIES

All cold injuries are connected to the reduction of peripheral circulation as the body attempts to reduce heat loss in the core. Various factors affect a person's susceptibility to cold injuries. Obviously low temperatures are needed but wind chill, wet skin, exposed skin, previous cold injuries, tight clothes, cramped position, body type, sex (woman suffer less than men), dehydration, calorific intake, diabetes and some medications can all be influences.

Frostbite

Watch keepers or survivors in open liferafts are particularly prone to tissue fluids freezing in localized areas of the body. It usually occurs at the body's extremities – fingers, toes, ears etc. The depth of damage is graded like burns into first degree (frostnip), second degree (superficial frostbite), third degree (severe frostbite) and fourth degree (deep frostbite). The signs are:
• Cold with pale to waxy white skin colour.
• Initial tingling and stiffness changing to numbness and anaesthesia.
• Skin changes from hard, rubbery top layer to wooden all the way through.
• Finally, freezing of muscle and/or bone.

To reduce the risk of frostbite, all watch keepers should:
• Wear protective clothing.
• Reduce lookout periods in very cold weather and watch each other's condition.
• Wriggle nose and cheeks, and exercise hands and feet to keep circulation going.
• Not smoke as this reduces peripheral blood circulation.

At the first sign of frostbite immediate steps should be taken to re-warm the frozen parts and to get out of the wind.
• Do not massage affected area once signs of frostbite have appeared.
• Warm the area by:
    ◦ blowing warm air on it
    ◦ holding a hand against it
    ◦ placing hands under armpits etc.

In theory, if you cannot guarantee that the tissue will stay warm, third and fourth degree frostbite should not be re-warmed. Once the tissue is frozen harm has already been done and keeping it frozen will not cause significant additional damage. On the other hand refreezing after warming can cause extensive damage and may result in loss of tissue. On a liferaft unless help is nearby you probably do not have much choice.

If a person is hypothermic as well as frostbitten, the first concern is body core re-warming. Do not re-warm frostbitten areas until the body core is almost normal.

When treatment has been ineffective skin dies and becomes black. If this occurs, dry dressings should be applied to the affected parts.

Chilblains

These are caused by repeated exposure of the skin to temperatures above freezing but below 16°C (60°F). Redness and itching affect the area and the skin swells and becomes bluish red. Chilblains are found particularly on cheeks, ears, fingers and toes of women and children. Warming by breathing on them may help, though itching may be made worse. Do not massage the area. The cold causes permanent damage to the peripheral capillary bed and the redness and itching will return with re-exposure.

Immersion foot (trench foot)

Immersion foot is similar to chilblains. It occurs when:

- Local tissue temperature of the limbs (usually feet) remains sub normal but above freezing for prolonged periods.
- Exposed in a liferaft for several days if the feet are wet and immobile.
- Cold and usually, but not necessarily, immersed in cold water.
- Feet are immobile for prolonged periods with tight footwear.

The affected part will be:

- White, numb, cold and slightly swollen.
- If untreated, the skin tissue begins to die. Circulation can be permanently impaired and tissue damage can ultimately cause the loss of the limb.
- Hot, red, swollen and very painful with returning warmth.

Do not rub the skin when re-warming.

Every effort should be made to prevent immersion foot:

- Keep the liferaft as dry as possible.
- Keep feet warm and dry.
- Regularly exercise knee and ankle joints.
- Loosen shoelaces and raise feet.
- Remove shoes, warm feet under the armpits of others, but outside their clothes.
- Use spare clothes and plastic bags to wrap feet.
- Use TPAs to keep feet dry even with water in the raft.

HEAT ILLNESSES

In warm or tropical climates excessive exposure to the sun and heat can cause extremely bad cases of sunburn and hyperthermia (or heatstroke). Heat illnesses are the result of elevated body temperatures due to an inability to dissipate the body's heat and/or a decreased fluid level. Three levels of heat illness are likely in survival craft: heat cramps, heat exhaustion and, most serious of all, hyperthermia, which can kill. See Chapters 5 and 6 for methods of keeping cool and protected in a liferaft in hot weather.

Heat cramps

Often these are the first warning of heat exhaustion, they are a form of muscle cramp brought on by exertion and insufficient salt due to sweating. Action to take:
- Move patient to coolest part of the liferaft.
- Sponge with seawater.
- Unless fresh water is severely rationed replace salt and fluid with a commercial rehydration solution or mix 1 tablespoon of seawater with 400 ml (16 fl oz) fresh water (1 part seawater to 64 parts fresh water) and drink slowly over an hour.
- Stretch the affected muscle.
- Do not knead and pound as this may cause residual soreness.

Heat exhaustion

This occurs when fluid losses caused by sweating and respiration are greater than the body's internal fluid reserves. Lack of fluid causes the body to constrict blood vessels in the arms and legs. Signs and symptoms are:
- Sweating.
- Skin pale and clammy.
- Pulse fast and weak.
- Respiration rapid and shallow.
- Nausea and vomiting.
- Patient weak, dizzy, thirsty and possibly has blurred vision.

Treatment should be similar to that for fainting plus rehydration and rest. Action to take:
- Move patient to coolest part of the liferaft.
- Sit or lie the patient with their feet raised.
- Sponge with seawater.
- Unless fresh water is severely rationed, replace salt and fluid with a commercial rehydration solution or mix 1 tablespoon of seawater with 400 ml (16 fl oz) fresh water (1 part seawater to 64 parts fresh water) and drink slowly over an hour.

- Monitor carefully, and check that heat exhaustion does not become hyperthermia.
- Make the victim rest for at least a day.

Hyperthermia (heat stroke)

Hyperthermia is the opposite of but is similar to hypothermia in that it affects the body's core temperature. Key factors:
- Caused by working in the heat.
- The body cannot lose heat fast enough when fluid levels are low.
- Core temperature rises, leading to unconsciousness and possibly death.
- It can happen quickly.
- A victim can die if untreated.

The signs and symptoms of hyperthermia are:
- Hot skin: this is the key sign. It may be dry, or wet if the victim has just moved from heat exhaustion.
- Skin pale with flushed feverish face.
- Pulse rapid and strong.
- Respiration rapid and deep.
- Severe headache often with vomiting.
- Pupils may be dilated and unresponsive to light.
- Fainting, delirium or seizures.
- The patient may become comatose, especially if core temperature is above 41°C (105°F).

Efforts to reduce body temperature must begin **immediately.**
- Move patient to coolest part of the liferaft.
- Remove clothing.
- Sprinkle with seawater or cover extremities with wet blankets.
- Fan to increase air circulation and improve evaporation.
- Massage extremities vigorously to help propel cooled blood back to the core.
- Once cooled stop active cooling and cover.
- Monitor carefully, it may be necessary to re-cool victim several times before temperature stabilises.
- Unless fresh water is severely rationed replace salt and fluid with a commercial rehydration solution or mix 1 tablespoon of seawater with 400 ml (16 fl oz) fresh water (1 part seawater to 64 parts fresh water) and drink slowly over an hour.
- Make victim rest for at least a day.

SALT-WATER BOILS

These are caused by the skin becoming sodden with seawater over a period of days. Action to take:
- Do not squeeze or burst boils.
- Flush with fresh water.
- Apply an antiseptic ointment.
- Keep boils clean and cover with a dry dressing.
- Keep area as dry as possible to avoid chafing.

DRY MOUTH AND CRACKED LIPS

A common problem when water is limited. Action to take:
- Swill any water around mouth prior to swallowing.
- Suck a button, removed from clothing.
- Smear lips with cream or petroleum jelly to reduce cracking.

SWOLLEN LEGS

A common problem caused by long periods spent in a sitting position. It will subside without treatment after rescue.

CONSTIPATION

Liferaft rations do not produce a lot of waste products for the body to expel and bowel movements in consequence will not be as frequent as normal. Actual constipation is a common problem on a liferaft in the long term with a diet of fish and little water. Seaweed, if plenty of fresh water is available, will provide good roughage. Do not take a laxative, this will increase dehydration.

URINE RETENTION

This can be dangerous and everyone should be encouraged to urinate as soon as possible after they arrive in the liferaft, whilst the body is still hydrated. With water rationing, normal urine production will be much reduced, and urine will appear dark and smoky.

9

RESCUE

In the middle of the Pacific Ocean, watch keepers high up on the bridge of a large ship will not be paying the same attention to looking for other vessels, let alone liferafts, as they might in more frequented waters, unless they have already been alerted. While survival is necessary, rescue is the goal of everyone aboard a liferaft.

If you contacted someone before the yacht sank, you know help is coming. If an EPIRB was your only means of distress alerting, help should be on its way:
- within 5 minutes with an Inmarsat E or 406 MHz EPIRB with GPS
- up to 2 hours later with a 406 MHz EPIRB without GPS
- possibly never with only a 121.5/243 MHz beacon.

With no direct contact and no EPIRB your chances of rescue depend upon:
- how far offshore you are
- whether you left a Voyage Details Plan with anyone.

Even in wartime, when lookouts were particularly alert, there were many occasions when ships failed to spot lifeboats and liferafts within easy distance and even flares failed to attract attention. It is very difficult to spot a liferaft further than about 8 km (5 miles) from the air by eye alone, on a fine sunny day, much less far from a ship in bad weather or poor visibility.

As soon as you know that help is in the area you should use all the signalling equipment in the liferaft to indicate your position.

Once an aircraft or ship has been sighted, everyone in the liferaft will expect immediate rescue. This may not happen because a craft capable of recovering you might not be immediately available or there may be a higher priority.

You must maintain survival routines until the moment of rescue.

Do not despair if you are not immediately sighted or if a crewmember mistakes a star or the rising moon for a ship. It is vital for your mental health and that of everyone else in the liferaft to remain optimistic. It can never hurt to include a prayer to whichever deity you favour for your safe deliverance.

WHO MIGHT ARRIVE

Sailors should have some knowledge of search and rescue (SAR) capabilities and procedures for the sea areas through which they are passing. Unfortunately it is not always easy to get hold of this information for every area of the world.

SAR off the coasts of the United Kingdom

In Great Britain information about SAR assistance is given in the *Annual Summary of Admiralty Notices to Mariners* and this is shown overleaf in the flowchart.

HM Coastguard, a division of the MCA, is the authority responsible for initiating and co-ordinating all civil maritime SAR measures for vessels in their region. This area is bounded by latitudes 45° and 61° North, by 30° West and by the adjacent European Search and Rescue Regions. The area is subdivided into five maritime Search and Rescue Regions (SRR) each containing at least one Maritime Rescue Co-ordination Centre (MRCC) with additional Sub-Centres (MRSC), which all maintain a constant manned communications watch. MRCC Falmouth acts as the primary contact for Rescue Control Centres outside Europe, the link for Inmarsat alerts and all EPIRB alerts on 406, 121.5 and 243 MHz.

SAR off the coasts of the USA

The US Coast Guard (USCG) is the authority responsible for initiating and co-ordinating all civil maritime SAR for vessels in their region. This huge area includes the Caribbean and a large part of the northern Pacific Ocean. The area is subdivided into ten RCCs and one Sub-Centre (RSC San Juan). Each of these eleven rescue centres receives distress alerts directly. The USCG undertakes the majority of SAR operations themselves, though they do receive help from both the US Navy and US Air Force when they request it. Close to the coast, the USCG is augmented by the USCG Auxiliary. Details for SAR facilities in other countries in the world are detailed in Radio Lists issued by the UK Hydrographic Office and in publications issued by those other countries.

ATTRACTING THE ATTENTION OF RESCUE UNITS

The first indication of help at hand may be a message over your VHF, activation of the SART (Search and Rescue Transponder), sighting a craft or hearing an aircraft.

If you know rescue craft are in the vicinity it is important to use every means of attracting attention. Possible distances that search vessels may receive your signal, assuming highest quality equipment and good conditions, are:

Assistance given to distress vessels in the UK Search and Rescue Region

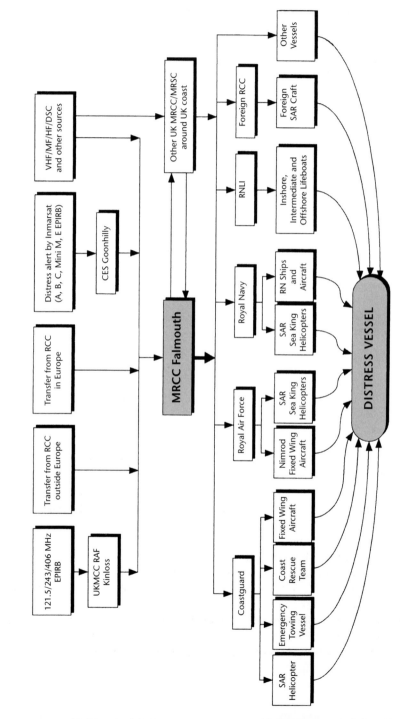

- EPIRB 121.5 MHz homing signal: line of sight.
- Liferaft light: 3 km (2 miles).
- Flares (SOLAS):
  - red parachute: 44 km (28 miles)
  - red handheld: 8 km (5 miles)
  - orange handheld smoke: 5 km (3 miles)
  - orange buoyant smoke: 10 km (6 miles)
- Radar reflector: depends greatly on how high it is mounted.
- SART: 16 km (10 miles).
- Signal Mirror: 16 km (10 miles).
- Signalling torch: 35 km (22 miles).
- Strobe light: 8 km (5 miles).
- VHF, hand held: 8 km (5 miles).
- Whistle: 2 km (less than 1 mile).

These distances may be much greater for SAR aircraft and will be reduced if the equipment is not of the best quality, or in bad weather with poor visibility.

EPIRB

With rescue near at hand your EPIRB should be attached outside the liferaft if it has a strobe light fitted, especially at night.

Pyrotechnics

Flares should not be used unless it is certain that help is nearby. Do not look directly at any flare as it may damage your vision, particularly at night.

Attracting attention

To attract attention use a red parachute rocket:
- fire slightly downwind; they are designed to turn into the wind
- aimed into the wind they may fail to gain altitude and be blown back aboard
- with low cloud, fire about 45° downwind so it burns under the cloud
- **Do not** fire when aircraft or helicopters are in the immediate area.

Pinpointing your position

Pinpoint your position when help is in sight with:
- red handheld flares in poor visibility, high winds or darkness
- orange buoyant or handheld smoke flares in daylight with good visibility and a light wind.
- Hold orange smoke and red handheld flares firmly downwind and clear of the raft, to prevent any hot ash hurting you or the liferaft.
- Throw a buoyant smoke signal into the water to leeward.

Signalling light

While it is almost impossible to use a heliograph to signal SOS in a liferaft the same is not true with a torch. A regularly flashing light is more likely to be sighted, such as repeated flashing of the Morse signal SOS (•••—-•••), than simply shining a torch in the direction of rescuers.

Signal mirror

A mirror is one of the most effective visual signals available in bright sunshine to attract attention. It is easiest to use when the sun is in the same direction as the target. Instructions for use should be included with the mirror:

- Raise the mirror close to your face.
- Sight the aircraft or vessel through the hole in the centre.
- Some sunlight should come through the hole and land on your face or clothing.
- Tilt the mirror until the reflection disappears through the hole while still seeing the target.
- At that point the sun will be reflected on aircraft or vessel.
- The movement of the survival craft will provide sufficient flashing effect.
- Be careful not to blind the pilot of an aircraft.

A heliograph or signal mirror is simple, non-mechanical and highly effective.

VHF

If you have a portable VHF in your liferaft it will enable you to talk to your rescuers before they arrive. It can also be used by SAR units fitted with VHF direction finding equipment to locate the liferaft.

Whistle

Whilst the primary use of a whistle is for survivors in the water, both to attract their attention and for them to alert others to their position, it can also be used to indicate the position of a liferaft to searching vessels. This may be particularly important in restricted visibility, when people are making a special effort to listen for any noise.

THE ARRIVAL OF FIXED WING AIRCRAFT

Fixed wing aircraft have a much greater range than helicopters and may be the first to find you. Unless you can alert overhead aircraft to your presence they may consider their search to be a failure and move on to another area.

Off the coasts of the United Kingdom SAR Nimrod MR2 aircraft fly between 100 and 1500 m (300 and 5000 ft), or below cloud, day or night, using a variety of search patterns. In other territories, altitudes and search patterns are very similar but a wide variety of aircraft are utilized. Aircrew fire a green flare when the aircraft makes a turn to start a new search leg and when they spot the survivors, to let them know they have been seen.

If you sight a green flare you must:

1 Fire one red flare.
2 Fire another red flare after one minute to allow the aircraft to line up on your bearing.
3 Fire a third flare if the aircraft appears to be badly off course.

There are a few points to note:
- Use any means at your disposal to attract attention.
- Do not aim the flares directly at the aircraft, particularly helicopters; it will not help you if you endanger them!
- Use a portable VHF if you have one available; many rescue aircraft can be contacted using Channel 16.

Fixed wing aircraft provide more than just verification that help is needed. They can:
- Provide an exact location of the distress to the shoreside authorities and ships in the vicinity.
- Guide rescue vessels and helicopters to the liferaft: invaluable in rough weather when wave heights are huge and a small craft can be hard to spot.
- Keep the liferaft under observation and provide reassurance.
- Mark the position of the survivors with a sonabuoy (a radio beacon about 45 cm [18 in] long by 12 cm [5 in] in diameter, with a flotation bag and aerial on top) to help guide the rescue craft.
- Drop survival equipment.

Droppable SAR apparatus

Survival equipment may be dropped from aircraft. There are stories of people in distress and urgent need of basic supplies who have failed to realise what they have just received from the skies. The British Royal Air Force SAR Nimrod MR2 fixed wing aircraft drop SAR apparatus upwind enabling it to drift downwind towards you. Known as ASRA (Air Sea Rescue Apparatus and previously called Lindholme Gear), it consists of:

- Three rigid cylindrical canisters linked by 550 m (600 yd) of orange coloured buoyant ropes.
- The long centre container holds an automatically inflating 10-person MS10 liferaft.
- The two identical canisters on either end each contain:
  - reverse osmosis manual watermaker x 1
  - water carriers x 3
  - small first aid kit x 1
  - signal mirror x 1
  - ground air codes, for use on dry land x 1
  - survival hoods x 5
  - headover scarves x 5
  - survival flip card x 1
  - survival rations x 6
  - drinking water pouches containing 250ml (1 cup) x 5
  - day/night distress flares x 3
  - whistle x 1
  - miniflares (8) and firing mechanism x 2
  - pocket knife x 1

You should:
- Manually deploy the sea anchor.
- Discard all empty outer containers by sinking.
- Secure all contents especially in rough seas.
- Do not unpack the inner containers until or unless the contents are required.

The aircraft may also drop a Dinghy Pair which are two canisters joined by 365 m (400 yd) of orange buoyant rope, each containing an automatically inflating MS10 liferaft

RESCUE BY HELICOPTER

The ultimate in quick-fix rescues are those undertaken by helicopters. The main type of helicopter used for SAR in the UK is the Sea King. These helicopters have an automatic hover control system and can effect rescues both at night and in fog where there are no visual hover references. The rescue can be dangerous, particularly in rough weather. A helicopter produces a very strong downdraft so the raft and its occupants will receive a severe buffeting. **Always** follow the instructions of the helicopter crew even if they differ from what you have learned in the past or what is written here.

- **Do not** touch winchman, stretcher or winch hook until these have been earthed.
- **Do not** secure any lines passed down.
- Grab a line using a glove or cloth to prevent rope burn.
- Assist the winchman by pulling on line as he approaches liferaft.
- **Do not** fire parachute flares when a helicopter is in the area.
- **Do not** transmit on the radio whilst winching is in progress.
- **Do not** stand up, unless or until you have to.
- **Do not** shine a light at the helicopter at night.
- Tie down everything and remove any aerials, SARTs etc. Even a small piece of paper ingested into a helicopter engine can cause a crash.
- Don lifejackets unless this would cause unjustified deterioration to the condition of an injured person.
- Deploy the liferaft sea anchor.
- Remove any liferaft canopy if possible.
- Rebalance the raft as each person is winched out.

The skipper of the liferaft should liaise with the winchman to decide in which order the survivors should be evacuated. Special devices for hoisting or lowering people may be used and these are described below.

Rescue sling

This is the most common method of getting survivors into a helicopter. UK SAR helicopters always use a double lift where a winchman is lowered with a strop for a survivor. When there are several survivors to be rescued, the winchman may take two strops with him. In this case, when he reaches the liferaft, the winchman will detach himself from the winch-hook and feed the survivors up to the helicopter two at a time.

If the winchman thinks survivors are cold and potentially hypothermic, he may elect to winch them in a horizontal position to minimise further injury. This is achieved with two strops, placing one under your armpits and the other behind the knees. If a single strop is supplied without a winchman, it must be used as follows:

1 Grasp the strop and put both arms and head through the loop.
2 Ensure the wide padded part is as high as possible across the back; the two sides are under the armpits and the wire is up in front of the face.
3 Pull toggle down as far as possible.

4 When ready, look up at the helicopter, put one arm out and give a clear 'thumbs up'.
5 Put both arms down beside the body.
6 On being winched up alongside the helicopter do nothing until instructed by the helicopter crew.

Other winch attachments

As an alternative to a rescue sling one of the following may be attached to the end of the winch cable:

- *Rescue basket*: climb into this, sit down and hold on.
- *Rescue net*: a conically shaped cage, open on one side; climb in, sit down and hold on.
- *Rescue litter*: designed for hoisting injured survivors.
- *Rescue seat*: can hoist two people at once. It looks like a three-pronged anchor with flat flukes or seats. Sit astride one or two of the seats and wrap your arms around the shank.

RESCUE BY SHIP

If a ship is going to rescue you, it is important to clear away any lines including the sea anchor and other gear that could cause entanglement. Survivors must don their lifejackets unless this could cause substantial deterioration in the condition of an injured person. The ship may approach so as to put the raft on its lee side and then drift down on you. Be careful of the raft being sucked into the propeller anywhere abaft the beam. Alternatively the ship may put a rescue craft or lifeboat into the water.

Boarding the ship may be by the liferaft being winched up with survivors aboard. You may have to climb aboard using ropes, a ladder or a scrambling net lowered over the side.

Remember that after any period in a liferaft, survivors are likely to be weakened; do not overestimate strength, take extra care.

Preparation for being taken in tow

If the rescue craft is small or the sea conditions are difficult, the liferaft may be towed to a place of safety before survivors are transferred. Actions to take:

- Use the painter or drogue line as a towline if they are in good condition.
- Attach a supplied line to the liferaft painter patch or bridle.
- Establish a simple communication system with the towing vessel.
- Pull in the sea anchor before towing commences.
- Once under way remain as still as possible to keep the liferaft balanced.
- Watch out for chafe or damage to the liferaft during the tow.
- Keep a knife ready in case the towline needs to be cut in an emergency.

LANDING AND BEACHING

You might reach land rather than be rescued and one of the watchkeeper's duties is to look carefully for any signs of land. There are many indicators that land is near in addition to the obvious sighting on the horizon. They are:

- Drifting vegetation or wood.
- Birds. (A single bird may be lost; repeated sightings may indicate nearby land.)
- The direction flocks of birds fly at dawn and dusk. This may indicate the direction of land as some sea birds roost on land.
- Wind, which frequently blows towards land by day and away from land at night.
- Very light coloured water. This indicates shallow water and nearby land. (Colour change only could be a continental shelf, hundreds of miles from land.)
- A greenish tint on the underside of a cloud layer in the tropics is often caused by coral reefs or lagoons.
- Light-coloured reflections on the underside of a uniform cloud layer in the Arctic, may indicate ice fields or snow-covered land. (Open water reflects dark grey.)
- Fixed cumulus cloud in a clear sky, or where other clouds are moving. This often hovers over or slightly downwind of an island.
- A change in the pattern of the swell, which may indicate a change of tide around an island.
- A decrease in swell, whilst the wind remains constant. This may indicate an island to windward, protecting the sea.
- The sound of surf: this carries well over water, and can be helpful at night, in fog, mist or rain.
- The smell of land; this can be very distinctive, especially after some time at sea.

Mirages can occur in any latitude but they are more common in the tropics, especially in the middle of the day. Be careful not to mistake a mirage for nearby land. Try altering your position, standing up or sitting down to check your sighting is real.

Landing

The greatest danger in any boat is not in the open ocean but near rocky or coral shores. Getting ashore safely in a liferaft is difficult especially in anything but calm conditions. Take your time before making an attempt, and remember:

- A liferaft is hard to manoeuvre, easy to rip.
- The crew are probably not in peak condition.

The easiest landing will be:
- A flat sloping sandy beach.
- The lee side of an island.
- Inside a small bay that will shelter you from the waves.
- In daylight.

If possible avoid:
- Shores with high cliffs
- Coral reefs
- Breaking surf
- Darkness.

If the shore looks unsuitable try to paddle to a better place. Go around to the leeward side of an island and look for gaps in the surf line. Head for the mouth of a freshwater stream where there will not be any coral. If the coast is inhabited try to attract attention before landing; the local inhabitants may be able to come out to get you. Alternatively they may direct you to a good landing spot. Unless it will clearly be an easy landing:
- Put on shoes, plenty of clothing and lifejackets to protect yourself from rocks and coral.
- Tie everything down to prevent it flying around.
- Hold on tightly or use a safety line to attach yourself to the raft.
- Sit outside any canopy, to aid escape easily in the event of capsize.
- Consider cutting off the canopy, but keep it for use ashore.
- Waves often arrive in sets of seven; time your landing to coincide with the smallest one.
- Stream the sea anchor to avoid surfing and prevent a capsize.
- In heavy surf consider filling the liferaft with water to make it more stable.
- Near surf, everyone should sit on the seaward side to maintain stability.

Approaching the shore

Paddle hard towards the beach between waves. Back paddle as hard as you can when the next breaking wave is catching you. If you are thrown out of the raft, hold on to the lifelines and stay with the raft as it is much more dangerous to swim ashore alone. Also your liferaft contains all your supplies; they may be needed ashore.

If you seem to be drifting away from the shore it may be because you are caught in a rip current or the outflow of a river. Do not fight it, paddle across it, they are not usually very wide. Once clear make for the shore.

As the raft nears the beach try to ride in on the crest of a large wave. Paddle or row hard and ride the wave as far up the beach as possible. Do not jump out of the raft until it has grounded.

Once grounded, be quick to get out and beach your craft. Drag the raft above the tide line.

ASHORE

The priorities once everyone is safely ashore will depend upon where you are, the time of year and the condition of all the other crewmembers. Surviving along the seashore is different from open water survival and is not covered by this book; this is when you will be glad you packed something like the SAS Survival Guide in your grab bag. Food and water are usually more abundant ashore and shelter easier to locate and construct. With the immediate problems of survival solved, rescue again becomes the priority.

It is important to make use of any and all possible methods of attracting attention including two methods that were not available in your liferaft. They are signal fires and ground to air signalling.

Signal fires

Establish signal fires as soon as possible. Ideally build three fires in a triangle at equal distances apart and keep them dry and maintained. Do not light the fires until you see an aircraft or vessel, unless fuel is abundant.

Create smoke to contrast with your background: for light smoke against dark earth or forest use green leaves, damp grass, seaweed etc; for dark smoke against snow or desert sand use rubber, such as bits of liferaft etc.

Ground to air signalling

Construct signs as large and as noticeable as possible, ideally 10 m (30 ft) for each letter, and each line 2 m (6 ft) wide. Make the letters in as clear an area as possible using a colour that contrasts with the ground. Use one of the following:

V   I require assistance
X   I require medical assistance.

Leaving the beaching area

Once the signalling fires and signs are organised and all the distress alerting equipment from aboard the liferaft has been made ready, you can consider the future. Explore the area for any clear signs of habitation or an obvious direction where help might be located. If there is nothing to indicate anyone nearby it may be better to stay where you landed, especially if food and water are available. If you do decide that all or one of you should go for help, where to go will be determined by any information you have gathered or knowledge of the area. If all else fails follow the coast or a waterway.

APPENDIX 1
VOYAGE DETAILS PLAN

Details of Vessel

Name of vessel:

Registered owner:

Where name displayed:

Official No: Sail or Fishing No:

Description of vessel

Type: motor ☐   sail ☐   Rig: schooner ☐   ketch ☐   sloop ☐   other _____

Make: Length of vessel: metres / feet

Colour of sails: Colour of topsides:

Colour of hull above waterline: Colour of hull below waterline:

Any special identifying features:

Engine type: No. of engines:

HP: Fuel capacity:

Dinghy make and model   Dinghy colour:

Captain of vessel

Name: Age:

Address:

Telephone: Mobile:

Nautical qualifications:

Any additional information:

Lifesaving equipment

Number of lifejackets: Colour of lifejackets:

Liferaft make and model: Liferaft colour:

Liferaft emergency pack: Grab bag ☐   Contents list attached ☐

Flares carried:

121.5 MHz EPIRB ☐   406 MHz EPIRB ☐   Inmarsat E EPIRB ☐   SART ☐

Radio and navigation equipment

Fixed VHF ☐   Portable VHF ☐   Short wave ☐   DSC distress alert ☐
Radio callsign: MMSI No:

Satellite System: Yes ☐   No ☐   Satellite model:

Satellite telephone No: _____

Radar ☐ GPS ☐ Echo sounder ☐

Planned trip

Date and time of departure: _____

Departure from: _____

Departure to: _____

Expected date and time of arrival: _____

Crew/passengers aboard

Number of persons aboard: _____

Name: _____ Age: _____

Address: _____

Name: _____ Age: _____

Address: _____

Name: _____ Age: _____

Address: _____

Name: _____ Age: _____

Address: _____

Name: _____ Age: _____

Address: _____

Name: _____ Age: _____

Address: _____

Name: _____ Age: _____

Address: _____

Additional Information: _____

_____

What to do if vessel is overdue

If no contact made by: _____ Call the Coastguard or Local Authority on: _____

_____

Notes: This Passage Plan has been left with you and only with you, as I know you can be relied upon to contact the number(s) above if necessary. If for any reason our departure is delayed I promise to phone you immediately so our expected arrival date can be changed. I also promise to phone you as soon as possible should there be any other change of plan and immediately upon our arrival at each stop.

If you need to contact us while we are under way: _____

_____

APPENDIX 2
MAYDAY VHF PROCEDURE

Motor/Yacht Serenity
November Hotel Golf Whisky 8
MMSI 366924365

IF THE VESSEL OR A PERSON IS IN GRAVE AND IMMINENT DANGER AND IMMEDIATE ASSISTANCE IS REQUIRED:

VHF (GMDSS)

- Check VHF is on. (If not depress green button on handset.)
- Remove handset from wall unit.
- Lift plastic lid, on wall unit, covering orange button.
- **PRESS AND HOLD ORANGE 'DISTRESS' BUTTON FOR 5 SECONDS.**
- Wait and listen.

On receipt of an acknowledgement or after 15 seconds:

- **PRESS RED CH 16 BUTTON.**
- If LOW is displayed on screen, press HI/LO button.
- **PRESS TRANSMIT BUTTON** and say slowly and clearly:

  MAYDAY, MAYDAY, MAYDAY

  This is Serenity, Serenity, Serenity.

  Mayday Serenity, November Hotel Golf Whisky Eight. MMSI 366924365

- **My position is . . .** (latitude and longitude using GPS)
  (IF YOU DON'T KNOW DON'T GUESS!)
- **I am . . .** (sinking, on fire etc)
- **I require immediate assistance**
- **I have . . .** (number of persons on board, any other information – drifting, flares fired etc)
- **Over**
- **RELEASE THE TRANSMIT BUTTON** and listen for an acknowledgement
- **KEEP LISTENING ON CH 16 FOR INSTRUCTIONS**

If an acknowledgement is not received, then repeat the distress call process from the beginning. Consider repeating the call on a different channel.

This is an example of a Mayday VHF procedure for a particular radio. Everything printed in tinted letters should be altered to reflect the equipment and details for your yacht. Any extra instruction, relevant to your particular equipment, should be included to enable a novice to make a successful Mayday call.

APPENDIX 3
MAYDAY SSB PROCEDURE

Motor/Yacht Blue Eagle
Juliet Bravo Oscar India 4

IF THE VESSEL OR A PERSON IS IN GRAVE AND IMMINENT DANGER AND IMMEDIATE ASSISTANCE IS REQUIRED:

- Check SSB is on. (If not depress black button on the top left.)
- Press the red button marked 2182 kHz.
- Press the button marked ALARM SIGNAL and hold for 30 to 60 seconds.
- Then remove handset from wall unit.
- **PRESS TRANSMIT BUTTON** and say slowly and clearly:

  MAYDAY, MAYDAY, MAYDAY

  This is Blue Eagle, Blue Eagle, Blue Eagle.

  Mayday Blue Eagle Juliet Bravo Oscar India 4

- **My position is . . .** (latitude and longitude using GPS)

  (IF YOU DON'T KNOW DON'T GUESS!)

- **I am . . .**(sinking, on fire etc)
- **I require immediate assistance**
- **I have . . .** (number of persons on board, any other information – drifting, flares fired, taking to liferaft etc)
- **Over**
- **RELEASE THE TRANSMIT BUTTON** and listen for an acknowledgement

If an acknowledgement is not received, then repeat the above procedure, particularly during the 3-minute silent period commencing at each hour and half-hour. Consider repeating the call on a different channel.

This is an example of a Mayday SSB procedure for a particular radio. Everything printed in tinted letters should be altered to reflect the equipment and details for your yacht. Any extra instruction, relevant to your particular equipment and/or the presence of a DSC controller, should be included to enable a novice to make a successful Mayday call.

APPENDIX 4
SOURCES OF SUPPLIES AND INFORMATION

GOVERNMENT, ORGANISATIONS ETC

AMSA (Australian Maritime Safety Authority)
Australian equivalent of MCA in the UK.
To register 406 MHz EPIRB: AusSAR, Australian Maritime Safety Authority, GPO Box 2181, Canberra ACT 2601, Australia
Tel: +(02) 6230 6811 Fax: +(02) 6230 6868
http://www.amsa.gov.au

COSPAS-SARSART
Download USA 406 MHz EPIRB registration form and learn lots more about the system.
NOAA SARSAT Beacon Registration:
E/SP3, RM 3320, FB-4, 5200 Auth Road, Suitland, MD 20746-4304, USA
Tel: +1 301 457 5678 or Toll free: +1 888 212 7283 Fax: +1 301 568 8649
http://www.cospas-sarsat.org and http://www.sarsat.noaa.gov

Cruising Association
A non-commercial UK organisation representing the interests of cruising sailors worldwide. It makes available up-to-date cruising information and promotes cruising interests.
CA House, 1 Northey Street, Limehouse Basin, London E14 8BT, UK
Tel: +44 (0)207 537 2828 Fax: +44 (0)207 537 2266
http://www.cruising.org.uk

IMO (International Maritime Organisation)
United Nations specialized agency responsible for improving marine safety and preventing pollution from ships.
4 Albert Embankment, London SE1 7SR, UK
Tel: +44 (0)20 7735 7611 Fax: +44 (0)20 7587 3210
http://www.imo.org

Inmarsat
Intergovernmental, global, mobile satellite communications operator, allowing voice, data, text and distress communication at sea.
For Inmarsat E EPIRB registration:
Inmarsat Ltd, Customer Activation Group, 99 City Road, London EC1Y 1AX, UK
Tel: +44 (0)207 728 1372 or switchboard +44 (0)207 728 1000
Fax: +44 (0)207 728 1142 or +44 (0)207 528 0898
http://www.inmarsat.org
http://www.inmarsat.org/safety

The Maritime and Coastguard Agency (MCA)
Government agency and controlling authority for British registered ships, responsible for marine safety, pollution prevention and responding to maritime emergency. Free download of Ship's Captain's Medical Guide and most M Notices. (MSN 1726 has a very useful list of drugs and how to use them etc.)
Spring Place, 105 Commercial Road, Southampton SO15 1EG, UK
Tel: +44 (0)2380 329100 Fax: +44 (0)2380 329404
To register a UK 406MHz EPIRB: The EPIRB Registry, MCA Southern Region (Falmouth), Pendennis Point, Castle Drive, Falmouth, Cornwall TR11 4WZ, UK
Tel: +1 (0)1326 211569 Fax: +1 (0)1326 319264
http://www.mcagency.org.uk

NOAA (National Oceanic and Atmospheric Administration)
Excellent Internet site for USA marine weather, hurricane warnings etc with links to other parts of the organisation.
http://www.noaa.gov - main site
http://www.nws.noaa.gov - National Weather Service home page

Royal National Lifeboat Institution (RNLI)
A British organisation to preserve life and promote safety at sea, using lifeboats manned by volunteers and funded by voluntary contributions. They offer a free Sea Safety check throughout the United Kingdom.
West Quay Road, Poole, Dorset BH15 1HZ, UK
Tel: +44 (0)1202 663174 To book an RNLI Sea Check: 0800 328 0600
http://www.rnli.org.uk

Royal Yachting Association (RYA)
The RYA is a UK organisation, a governing body representing the interests of everyone who goes on the water for pleasure. They run extensive training schemes including an excellent sea survival course.
RYA House, Romsey Road, Eastleigh, Hampshire SO50 9YA, UK
Telephone: +44 (0)23 8062 7400 Fax: +44 (0)23 8062 9924
http://www.rya.org.uk

The Stationery Office
Publishers of all Acts and Statutory Instruments in force in the UK and applicable to British registered vessels including pleasure vessels. Recent legislation is available via the website.
Publications Centre, PO Box 276, London SW8 5DT, UK
Tel: +44 (0)870 600 5522 Fax: +44 (0)870 600 5533
http://www.hmso.gov.uk/stat.htm

The United Kingdom Hydrographic Office
Admiralty Way, Taunton, Somerset TA1 2DN, UK
Tel: +44 (0)1823 337900 Fax: +44 (0)1823 284077
http://www.hydro.gov.uk

US Coast Guard

A huge site, lots of interesting and useful information on everything to do with the sea and safety. Some of the interesting places to go include:

http://www.uscg.mil - main site

http://www.uscg.mil/vtm/pages/rules.htm – download a copy of the Navigation Rules

http://www.uscg.mil/hq/g-o/g-opr/sar.htm – Home Page for US Coast Guard Search and Rescue

http://www.uscg.mil/hq/g-m/gmhome.htm – Marine Safety and Environmental Protection

GENERAL SAFETY EQUIPMENT MANUFACTURERS AND SUPPLIERS

BCB International Ltd

Survival and personal protection equipment.
Clydesmuir Road Industrial Estate, Cardiff CF24 2QS, UK
Tel: + 44 (0)2920 433700 Fax: +44 (0)29 20 433701
http://www.bcbin.com

Cruisermart

UK company with shops and mail order catalogue.
Unit 6, Waterloo Ind Est, Flanders Road, Hedge End, Southampton SO30 2QT, UK
Tel: +44 (0)1489 774444 Fax: +44 (0)1489 774445
http://www.cruisermart.co.uk

Landfall Navigation

Supplier and manufacturer of safety and navigation equipment including grab bag supplies and liferafts.
354 W. Putnam Ave, Greenwich, CT 06830, USA
Tel: +1 800 941 2219 or +1 203 661 3176 Fax: +1 203 661 9613
http://www.landfallnavigation.com

West Marine

Comprehensive chandlery well used to international customers (freephone from many countries). West adviser offers useful information on choosing equipment. Own liferaft made by Zodiac.
P.O. Box 50070, Watsonville, CA 95077-0070, USA
Tel: USA: (800) BOATING UK 0800-895473 International +1 831 761 4800
Fax: +1 831 761 4020
http://www.westmarine.com

YBW Marine Store
*British online shop part of IPC magazine site with UK weather and tidal informa-
tion.*
The Bothy, Lower Gardens, Wasing Park, Aldermaston, Berkshire RG7 4NG, UK
Tel: +44 (0)118 971 0125 Fax: +44 (0)118 971 0155
http://www.ybw-marine-store.com

DISTRESS EQUIPMENT MANUFACTURERS AND SUPPLIERS

ACR
Epirbs, ELTs, PLBs, VHF Radios, SARTs, survivor location lights.
Head Office: 5757 Ravenswood Road, Ft Lauderdale, FL 33312, USA
Tel: USA +1 954 981 3333 UK +44 (0)1590 682282
Fax: USA +1 954 983 5087 UK +44 (0)1590 683828
http://www.acrelectronics.com

Fastnet Radio
Inmarsat E manufacturers.
Rödingsmarkt 31-33, 20459 Hamburg, GERMANY
Tel: +49 40 36 98 98 0 Fax: +49 40 36 98 98 10
http://www.fastnet.de

ICS Electronics Ltd
Marine safety products including Inmarsat E Epirbs, GMDSS systems, Navtex.
Unit V, Rudford Industrial Estate, Ford, Arundel, West Sussex BN18 0BD, UK
Telephone: +44 (0)1903 731101   Fax: +44 (0)1903 731105
http://www.icselectronics.co.uk

Navtec GmbH
Inmarsat E manufacturers.
Flughafen Berlin-Schönefeld, D-12521 Berlin, Germany
Tel: +49 30 60 91 82 24 Fax : +49 30 60 91 82 23
http://www.navtec.de

Mcmurdo Pains-Wessex
Emergency electronics (EPIRB, VHF, SART), flares and survivor location lights.
Silver Point, Airport Service Road, Portsmouth, Hampshire PO3 5PB, UK
Tel: +44 (0)23 9262 3900 Fax: +44 (0)23 9262 3998
http://www.pwss.com

PUR Division Recovery Engineering Inc
Portable hand-operated emergency watermakers.
9300 North 75th Avenue, Minneapolis, Minnesota 55428, USA
Tel: 800 845 7873 or +1 612 541 1313 Fax: +1 612 541 1230
http://www.purwater.com

Sartech Engineering Ltd
Marine safety sales and servicing, including Kanard and McMurdo EPIRBs and SARTs.
80 Brighton Road, Lower Kingswood, Tadworth, Surrey KT20 6SY, UK
Tel +44 (0)1737 832237 Fax: +44 (0)1737 833903
http://www.sartech.co.uk

LIFERAFT MANUFACTURERS AND DISTRIBUTORS

Avon Inflatables Ltd
Dafen, Llanelli, Carmarthenshire SA14 8NA, UK
Tel: +44 (0)1554 882000 Fax: +44 (0)1554-882039
http://www.avonmarine.com

Ocean Safety
Distributors of Lifeguard liferafts. Also suppliers of a full range of safety equipment and service agents for a wide range of liferafts.
Saxon Wharf, Lower York Street, Southampton, SO14 5QF, UK
Tel: +44 (0)23 8072 0800 Fax: +44 (0)23 8072 0801
http://www.oceansafety.com

RFD Ltd
Kingsway, Dunmurry, Belfast BT17 9AF, Northern Ireland
Tel: +44 (0) 28 9030 1531 Fax: +44 (0) 28 9062 1765
http://www.rfd.co.uk

Switlik Parachute Company
1325 E State St, Trenton, NJ 08607-1328 USA
Tel: +1 609 587 3300 Fax: +1 609 586 6647
http://www.switlik.com

Viking
Head Office: P.O. Box 3060, 6710 Esbjerg V, Denmark
Tel: UK +44 (0)1603 767677 USA +1 305 374 5115
Fax: UK +44 (0)1603 766700 USA +1 305 374 1535
http://www.viking-life.com

Winslow Liferaft Company
11700 SW Winslow Drive, Lake Suzy, FL 34269 USA
Tel: +1 800 838 3012 or +1 941 613 6666   Fax: +1 941 613 6677
http://www.winslowliferaft.com

Zodiac
Zodiac International, 2 Rue Maurice Mallet, 92130 Issy-Les-Moulineaux, France
Tel: UK +44 (0)1604 497637   USA +1 410 643 4141
Fax: UK +44 (0)1604 497638 USA +1 410 643 4491
http://www.zodiac.com

OTHER MANUFACTURERS AND SUPPLIERS

BCB Ltd
Medical supplier, both drugs and equipment.
Moorland Road, Cardiff CF24 2YL, UK
Tel: +44 (0)2920 464464 Fax: +44 (0)2920 481100
http://www.bcb.ltd.uk

J L Darling Corp
All-weather writing paper and pens, including Dura Waterproof Rite paper for use in photocopiers and laser printers.
2614 Pacific Highway East, Tacoma, WA 98424, USA
Tel: +1 253 922 5000 Fax: +1 253 922 5300
http://www.riteintherain.com/

Lat.26 Inc
Waterproof paper for use in inkjet and bubble jet printers (ink becomes waterproof).
P. O. Box 833, Lake Arrowhead, CA 92352, USA
Tel: +1 800 305 0036
http://www.lat26inc.com

WeatherWriter
All-weather writing paper and pens including Fisher pressurized pens, and Zecom waterproof paper for use in photocopiers and laser printers.
VIP: Pettaugh, Stowmarket, Suffolk IP14 6AX, UK
Tel: +44 (0)1473 890285 Fax: +44 (0)1473 890764
http://www.weatherwriter.com

SURVIVAL SITES ON THE INTERNET

http://www.equipped.org
Doug Ritter's Equipped to Survive site with information on outdoor gear, survival equipment and survival techniques.

http://www.aircav.com
Air Cavalry site mainly about helicopters, and it includes a book on survival.

http://www.ussartf.org
US Search and Rescue Task Force, a private volunteer organisation on the east coast of the USA. The site contains excellent search and rescue and disaster related information.

http://www.vnh.org/StandardFirstAid/toc.html
US Navy digital library of naval and military medicine; it contains a lot of very useful first aid information available to anyone.

INDEX